British History
General Editor:

Eugenio Biagir
D.G. Boyce *The Irish Question and Br*
Keith M. Brown *Kingdom or Pro*
Union, 16
A.D. Carr *Medieval Wales*
Eveline Cruickshanks *The Glorious Revolution*
Anne Curry *The Hundred Years War (2nd edn)*
Susan Doran *England and Europe in the Sixteenth Century*
Seán Duffy *Ireland in the Middle Ages*
David Gladstone *The Twentieth-Century Welfare State*
Brian Golding *Conquest and Colonisation: the Normans in Britain, 1066–1100 (rev. ed*
Sean Greenwood *Britain and the Cold War, 1945–91*
David Harkness *Ireland in the Twentieth Century: Divided Island*
Ann Hughes *The Causes of the English Civil War (2nd edn)*
I.G.C. Hutchison *Scottish Politics in the Twentieth Century*
Ronald Hutton *The British Republic, 1649–1660 (2nd edn)*
T.A. Jenkins *Disraeli and Victorian Conservatism*
T.A. Jenkins *Sir Robert Peel*
H.S. Jones *Victorian Political Thought*
D.E. Kennedy *The English Revolution, 1642–1649*
Christine Kinealy *The Great Irish Famine*
David Loades *The Mid-Tudor Crisis, 1545–1565*
John F. McCaffrey *Scotland in the Nineteenth Century*
A.P. Martinich *Thomas Hobbes*
Roger Middleton *The British Economy since 1945*
W.M. Ormrod *Political Life in Medieval England, 1300–1450*
Richie Ovendale *Anglo-American Relations in the Twentieth Century*
Ian Packer *Lloyd George*
Keith Perry *British Politics and the American Revolution*
Murray G.H. Pittock *Scottish Nationality*
Murray G.H. Pittock *Jacobitism*
A.J. Pollard *The Wars of the Roses (2nd edn)*
David Powell *British Politics and the Labour Question, 1868–1990*
Richard Rex *Henry VIII and the English Reformation*
G.R. Searle *The Liberal Party: Triumph and Disintegration, 1886–1929 (2nd edi*
John Stuart Shaw *The Political History of Eighteenth-Century Scotland*
W.M. Spellman *John Locke*
William Stafford *John Stuart Mill*
Bruce Webster *Medieval Scotland*
Ann Williams *Kingship and Government in Pre-Conquest England*
Ian S. Wood *Churchill*
John W. Young *Britain and European Unity, 1945–99 (2nd edn)*
Paul Ziegler *Palmerston*

Please note that a sister series, *Social History in Perspective*, is available
covering the key topics in social and cultural history.

British History in Perspective
Series Standing Order: ISBN 0–333–71356–7 hardcover/ISBN 0–333–69331–0 paperback

You can receive future titles in this series as they are published by placing a standin
order. Please contact your bookseller or, in case of difficulty, write to the address
below with your name and address, the title of the series and the ISBN quoted abov

Customer Services Department, Macmillan Distribution Ltd
Houndmills, Basingstoke, Hampshire RG21 6XS, England

History of Ireland
D. G. Boyce **The Irish Question and British Politics, 1868–1996 (2nd edn)**
Seán Duffy **Ireland in the Middle Ages**
David Harkness **Ireland in the Twentieth Century: Divided Island**

History of Scotland
Keith M. Brown **Kingdom or Province? Scotland and the Regal Union, 1603–1715**
John F. McCaffrey **Scotland in the Nineteenth Century**
Bruce Webster **Medieval Scotland**

History of Wales
A. D. Carr **Medieval Wales**
J. Gwynfor Jones **Early Modern Wales, c.1525–1640**

Further titles are in preparation

Please note that a sister series, *Social History in Perspective*, is now available. It covers the key topics in social, cultural and religious history.

British History in Perspective
Series Standing Order
ISBN 0–333–71356–7 hardcover
ISBN 0–333–69331–0 paperback
(*outside North America only*)

You can receive future titles in this series as they are published by placing a standing order. Please contact your bookseller or, in case of difficulty, write to us at the address below with your name and address, the title of the series and the ISBN quoted above.

Customer Services Department, Macmillan Distribution Ltd
Houndmills, Basingstoke, Hampshire RG21 6XS, England

BRITISH DECOLONIZATION, 1946–1997

When, Why and How did the British Empire Fall?

W. DAVID MCINTYRE

Professor of History,
University of Canterbury,
Christchurch, New Zealand

© W. David McIntyre 1998

All rights reserved. No reproduction, copy or transmission of
this publication may be made without written permission.

No paragraph of this publication may be reproduced, copied or
transmitted save with written permission or in accordance with
the provisions of the Copyright, Designs and Patents Act 1988,
or under the terms of any licence permitting limited copying
issued by the Copyright Licensing Agency, 90 Tottenham Court Road,
London W1P 9HE.

Any person who does any unauthorised act in relation to this
publication may be liable to criminal prosecution and civil
claims for damages.

The author has asserted his right to be identified as
the author of this work in accordance with the Copyright,
Designs and Patents Act 1988.

First published 1998 by
MACMILLAN PRESS LTD
Houndmills, Basingstoke, Hampshire RG21 6XS
and London
Companies and representatives throughout the world

ISBN-13: 978-0-333-64437-9   hardback
ISBN-10: 0-333-64437-9   hardback
ISBN-13: 978-0-333-64438-6   paperback
ISBN-10: 0-333-64438-7   paperback

A catalogue record for this book is available from the British Library.

This book is printed on paper suitable for recycling and made from
fully managed and sustained forest sources.

Typeset by Footnote Graphics, Warminster, Wilts

Printed & bound in Great Britain by
Antony Rowe Ltd, Chippenham and Eastbourne

Published in the United States of America 1998 by
ST. MARTIN'S PRESS INC.,
Scholarly and Reference Division,
175 Fifth Avenue, New York, N.Y. 10010

ISBN 0–312–21307–7

CONTENTS

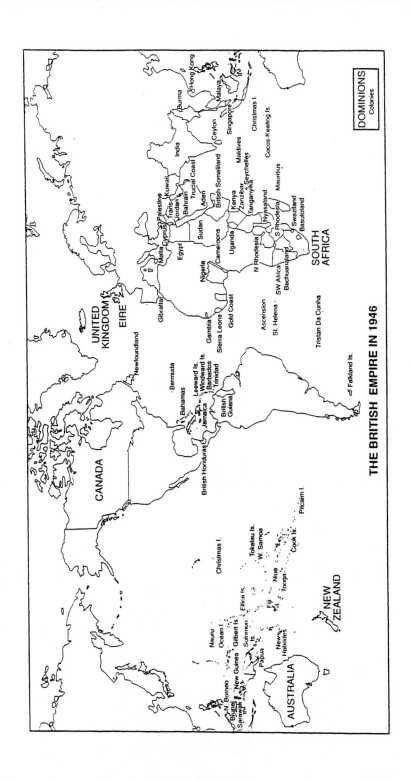

THE BRITISH EMPIRE IN 1946

DOMINIONS
Colonies

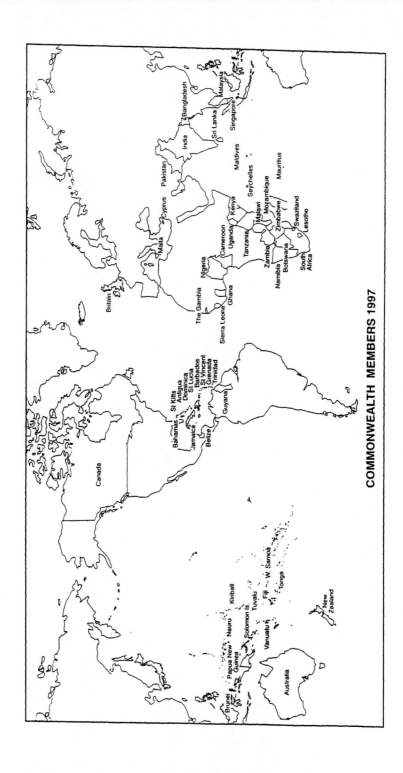

COMMONWEALTH MEMBERS 1997

TABLE OF INDEPENDENCE DATES

1946	Mar 22	Transjordan [Jordan from 1949]
1947	Aug 14	Pakistan
	Aug 15	India
1948	Jan 4	Burma [Myanmar from 1989]
	Feb 9	Ceylon [Sri Lanka from 1972]
	May 14	Palestine [Israel]
1951	Dec 24	Libya
1956	Jan 1	Sudan
1957	Mar 6	Gold Coast [Ghana]
	Aug 31	Malaya [part of Malaysia from 1963]
1960	Jun 31	British Somaliland [part of Somalia, 1 July]
	Aug 10	Cyprus
	Oct 1	Nigeria
1961	Apr 27	Sierra Leone
	Jun 1	Northern Cameroons [as part of Nigeria]
	Jun 19	Kuwait
	Oct 1	Southern Cameroons [as part of Cameroon]
	Dec 9	Tanganyika [Tanzania from 1964]
1962	Jan 1	Western Samoa
	Aug 6	Jamaica
	Aug 31	Trinidad and Tobago
	Oct 9	Uganda
1963	Sep 16	North Borneo [Sabah] ⎫
		Sarawak ⎬ [as part of Malaysia]
		Singapore ⎭
	Dec 10	Zanzibar [united in Tanzania from 1964]
	Dec 12	Kenya
1964	Jul 6	Nyasaland [Malawi]
	Sep 21	Malta GC
	Oct 24	Northern Rhodesia [Zambia]
1965	Feb 18	The Gambia
	Jul 26	Maldives
	Aug 9	Singapore

1966	May 26	British Guiana [Guyana]
	Sep 30	Bechuanaland [Botswana]
	Oct 4	Basutoland [Lesotho]
	Nov 30	Barbados
1967	Nov 29	Aden [South Yemen]
1968	Feb 1	Nauru
	Mar 12	Mauritius
	Sep 6	Swaziland
1970	Jun 4	Tonga
	Oct 10	Fiji
1971	Aug 15	Bahrain
	Sep 3	Qatar
	Dec 2	United Arab Emirates
	Dec 16	Bangladesh [seceded from Pakistan]
1973	Jul 10	Bahamas
1974	Feb 7	Grenada
	Feb 16	Papua New Guinea
1976	Jun 29	Seychelles
1978	Jul 7	Solomon Islands
	Oct 1	Ellice Islands [Tuvalu]
	Nov 3	Dominica
1979	Feb 22	St Lucia
	Jul 12	Gilbert Islands [Kiribati]
	Oct 27	St Vincent and the Grenadines
1980	Apr 18	Southern Rhodesia [Zimbabwe]
	Jul 30	New Hebrides [Vanuatu]
1981	Sep 21	Belize [British Honduras to 1973]
	Nov 1	Antigua and Barbuda
1983	Sep 19	St Kitts and Nevis
1984	Jan 1	Brunei Darassalam
1990	Mar 21	Southwest Africa [Namibia]
1997	Jul 1	Hong Kong [returned to the People's Republic of China]

PREFACE

In this book I try to do three things: to provide a concise narrative of the sequence of decolonization; to summarize, briefly, the debate about why it happened; and to consider what was distinctive about the way the events unfolded. Because the main landmarks are so recent – indeed they took place in my own life-time – the editor's invitation to contribute to this series induced unusual introspection. Was I part of the last imperial generation, or the first post-imperial generation? As a young teenager, I stood in Oxford Street to watch the Victory Parade in 1946, with its array of 'colonial contingents', but I never set foot in a British colony before its independence. At school and university, I do not recall being taught anything about the British Empire. However, my head-master, a distinguished historian, had been professor of history at the University of Rangoon in the 1920s and 1930s and he fascinated sixth formers by his frequent asides about 'When I was in Burma ... ' Otherwise, my awareness of the British Empire was first aroused by quite disparate manifestations. First, in stamp collecting I became aware that 'British colonials' were more valuable and decorative than 'French colonials', which were legion. Secondly, the locomotives which hauled me off to school were mainly of the LMS Jubilee class, eighty-five of which were named after imperial dependencies or provinces numbered (as I later came to realize) in a quite proper constitutional order. Thirdly, street names commemorating far-away battles excited curiosity. How-ever, it was not until post-graduate work in American history at an American university in the 1950s that I studied any 'colonial history'. My first whiff of 'decolonization' (as opposed to the thirteen colonies version) came from some African fellow-students who, in 1955, intro-duced themselves with great joviality as hailing from the Gold Coast – 'which is a British colony; but not for long!' By the time I completed a Ph.D. at the London School of Oriental and African Studies in 1959, the 'Wind of Change' was gusting strongly. A subsequent career teach-ing mainly Colonial and Commonwealth history has involved the chastening experience of seeing all my lectures and writings rapidly overtaken by events. And comfort is not in sight. Any temptation to imagine that what appears below can be a settling of accounts is qualified by the realization that, as the last flags come down over distant enclaves, the debate about decolonization has hardly begun. This is offered as a brief introduction to it.

I wish to acknowledge the support over many years of the University of Canterbury, especially the University Library and the History Department. Sam Adshead, Ian Campbell, Ian Catanach and Chris Connolly kindly commented on an early draft. Judy Robertson must be thanked for her word-processing and managerial skills, and my admiration is unbounded for Marcia, who mastered voice-recognition and talked my scribble into text.

W. David McIntyre
Christchurch

INTRODUCTION: THE EMPIRE IN 1946 AND DECOLONIZATION

The British Empire in 1946

On 8 June 1946 it was 'V-Day' in Britain. A year and a month after the end of the war in Europe, they held the Victory Parade. For two hours the King and Emperor, George VI, took the salute in The Mall. Below him, beside the podium, sat Clem Attlee, the prime minister, Winston Churchill, leader of the opposition, Mackenzie King, the Canadian prime minister, and Jan Smuts, the South African prime minister. Deputies for the Australian and New Zealand prime ministers sat further back. On the other side of the podium sat the Chiefs of Staff.

The Marching Column was headed by contingents from eighteen allied countries, led by the Americans. The Soviet Union, Poland and Yugoslavia had declined their invitations. Included among the allies were Egypt, Sudan, Iran, Iraq and Transjordan, which were all under varying degrees of British occupation, part of what has been termed the 'informal empire'. Next came large contingents from the Dominions – Canada, Australia, New Zealand and South Africa – followed by Southern Rhodesia (a quasi-Dominion) and Newfoundland (a former Dominion). Then came detachments from India and Burma, plus colourful troops from Indian Princely States, and the Gurkhas. These were followed by numerous colonial contingents, the largest from Africa – from West Africa, from East and Central Africa, and from the High Commission Territories in the south. They also came from Gibraltar, Malta, and Cyprus; from Palestine and Aden; from Ceylon, Malaya, Sarawak, North Borneo and Hong Kong; from the West Indies, Bermuda, St Helena and the Falkland Islands; from Mauritius and Seychelles, and from Fiji, Tonga, the Solomon Islands and the Gilbert and Ellice Islands. Only after this allied and imperial display did the

1

much more numerous representatives of Britain's own armed and civilian services make their salute. The parade was a visible symbol of the world's greatest empire at the peak of its territorial power.

The order of march down The Mall mirrored a conventional order of seniority among more than sixty countries which made up the British Commonwealth and Empire.[1] Pride of place was always accorded to the self-governing Dominions – so designated as a group since 1907. The Dominion of Canada was a confederation of provinces from the Atlantic to the Pacific dating from mid-Victorian times. Newfoundland, the oldest colony, having given up Dominion status in 1933, was now ruled by commissioners and was negotiating for admission to Canada. The Commonwealth of Australia had been created in 1901. New Zealand had stayed aloof from this, and was styled Dominion in 1907. The Union of South Africa was formed in 1910. Southern Rhodesia, which might have joined it, had opted in 1922 to become a self-governing colony. The three High Commission Territories, adjacent to, or surrounded by, the Union – Basutoland, Bechuanaland and Swaziland – were coveted by South Africa, but remained British protectorates. Southwest Africa was a League of Nations Mandate Territory ruled by South Africa. These Dominions were independent nations, members of the United Nations, but still linked to Britain in varying degrees by the Crown, trade, investment, migration, sport, and culture. One of their number, Eire, was absent from the parade, as it had been absent from recent imperial conferences and from the allied cause. As neutrals in the war, the Southern Irish had infuriated loyalists, but were still externally associated with the Commonwealth, treated as a Dominion, and there were those who hoped that this would continue.

After the Dominions, the Indian Empire, the most populous dependency, once the 'jewel in the Imperial Crown', was now scarcely governable and seemingly on the verge of revolt. The Viceroy, Field Marshal Wavell, could not afford to be away at the parade in London. He ruled over the central Government of India, eleven Provinces and over six hundred Princely States, governed by their own rulers with British Advisers. Self-government had been promised since 1917, Dominion status since 1929; ministerial government had been granted to the Provinces in 1937, and independence (inside or outside the Commonwealth) had been promised in 1942 to be achieved after the war. However, Hindus and Muslims had become so irreconcilable that there were obstinate demands from some quarters for a separate Muslim state of Pakistan. Three weeks before the Victory Parade, a Cabinet mission, which had spent nearly two months in India, published its proposals for a scheme to preserve India's unity in a three-tier polity comprising an All-India Union, with Federal Groups, and Provinces or States. Only a week before the Parade, the Viceroy, predicting the possibility of violent uprising, requested orders as to whether he should plan to scuttle or stay. Burma had been part of the Indian Empire, but had been detached since 1937, granted independence by Japanese conquerors in 1943, reoccupied in 1945, and promised eventual equal status to the Dominions. Ceylon (which, as one of the premier colonies under the Colonial Office, was quite separate from India) also aspired to Dominion status, the acronym of which had become the slogan every-one knew equated with the initials of the Sinhalese leader Don Stephen Senanayake (known as DS). A ministerial system of government, announced a month before the Victory Parade, fell short of Dominion status and some violence and unrest followed.

In contrast to the position in South Asia, where the British were clearly on the back foot, in Southeast Asia after the war they were in a newly expansive mood. In the wake of Japan's surrender, Malaya and North Borneo were re-occupied, and British troops also went on to occupy southern French Indo-China and the Netherlands East Indies. In March 1946, a Commissioner-General under the Foreign Office had been appointed to co-ordinate British relations with Thailand, Indo-China and the East Indies. In the month before the Victory Parade, the Colonial Office had also sent a Governor-General to Malaya with overall control of the British dependencies in the region, where major changes were under way. Malaya was potentially the prime dollar earner of the Empire because of its rubber and tin, and the rulers of the Malay States (which had always been Protected States on the Indian States model) had been forced after the war to give up, for the first time, full powers and jurisdiction to the Crown, and they were joined in a new Malayan Union. In northern Borneo, two former private colonies, which had been overrun by the Japanese, were about to come under official rule. Sarawak and British North Borneo (to which Labuan Island was added) would become new Crown colonies in July 1946. Brunei remained a Protected State. Singapore had been made a separate Crown colony, which also included the Cocos-Keeling Islands and Christmas Island in the Indian Ocean. There were those who deprecated these new arrangements and looked to a future Malayan Dominion.

Further north, Hong Kong, recently recovered from Japanese in-vaders, remained the sole relic of Britain's once dominant position on the China Coast, which had included the International Settlement of Shanghai and steamships in the main rivers. But the naval base at

Wei-hai-Wei had been given up in 1930 and extra-territorial rights in treaty ports surrendered in 1943. While post-war Hong Kong would flourish and grow, this was soon on the sufferance of the People's Republic of China.

In the oldest part of the colonial empire, the West Indies, Dominion status was also seen as the goal, but only on the basis of a federation for which preliminary meetings had already been called. It was not to be contemplated that individual islands would ever qualify for independence, though Barbados, Jamaica and Trinidad had long-standing representative institutions, as had British Guiana on the South American mainland. The other Caribbean colonies, which also had some measure of representative institutions, were all very small and poor. These included British Honduras (in Central America), the Leeward Islands (comprising Antigua, St Kitts-Nevis-Anguilla, Monserrat, and the Virgin Islands), and the Windward Islands (comprising Dominica, St Lucia, St Vincent and Grenada). The Bahamas were regarded as standing apart from the West Indies group. Isolated in the Atlantic lay Bermuda and St Helena (with Ascension and Tristan da Cunha). The informal empire in Latin America, in which Argentina had once been dubbed the 'Seventh Dominion', was rapidly succumbing to American competition and nationalist economic ambition.

The biggest swathe of colonial dependencies lay in Africa, in the lands between the Cape and Cairo. The Anglo-Egyptian Sudan, the largest in area, was the unique 'hobby colony' of the Foreign Office. The Colonial Office had charge of three groups of colonies and protectorates which, being so different in geography, history and ethos, had been kept in separate compartments. Now, through the possibilities of the Colonial Development and Welfare Acts, they were beginning to be viewed as vast tropical estates whose development would bolster the British economy. In West Africa, the most 'advanced' was the relatively prosperous cocoa-producing Gold Coast; the most populous was the vast palm-rich land of Nigeria. Sierra Leone and tiny Gambia were seen as less important charges. In East Africa, Kenya, Uganda and Tanganyika shared post, telegraph, railway, and harbour administrations and an East African High Commission had been proposed in 1945 to co-ordinate these services. While the white settlers of the Kenya Highlands had been given a measure of self-government and aspired to Closer Union and Dominion status, the official guardians of the African majorities in Uganda and Tanganyika had always resisted such moves. Tanganyika, as a UN Trust Territory, presented a special problem of accountability. In Central Africa, the self-governing colony of Southern

Rhodesia aspired to lead another Dominion by amalgamation with Northern Rhodesia and its rich copper belt. Senior officials in London favoured such unifications and a Central African Council, which also included Nyasaland, had been created during the war, but British Governments had held back, as yet, from permitting a Central African Dominion. Off the east coast lay Zanzibar, another protectorate, and in the Indian Ocean were the island colonies of Mauritius and the Seychelles. Relations with the Sultanate of the Maldives were conducted by the Governor of Ceylon.

Historically the last area to be absorbed into the imperial orbit was the largely informal empire in the Middle East. The opening of the Suez Canal, in 1869, provided a quicker, alternative, route to India and the Far East than that round the Cape of Good Hope. The colonies of Gibraltar and Malta protected the line-of-communication through the Mediterranean. Cyprus had been acquired initially, on lease from the Ottoman Empire. Port Said and Alexandria were imperial ports by virtue of treaty relations with the Egyptian Government, and in the 1939–45 War the Suez Canal Zone had become Britain's powerhouse in the region. Palestine and Transjordan, taken from the Turks in the 1914–18 war, were made Mandates under the League of Nations. Shortly before the Victory Parade in 1946, the Mandate in Transjordan had ended and its ruler recognized as king. At the southern end of the Red Sea the Suez route was guarded by Aden (transferred from India to the Colonial Office in 1937), and British Somaliland on the Horn of Africa. In the post-war years, former Italian Somaliland, Eritrea and parts of Ethiopia were also under British military occupation and a unified Somalia was being contemplated. In the Arabian/Persian Gulf, Iraq was a British creation from the 1914–18 war, and host to two air bases. At Abadan, in Iran, the largest oil refinery in the world gave rise to a virtual colony. Long-standing treaty relations with small Gulf States like Kuwait, Bahrain, Qatar, Dubai and Abu Dhabi, involved British forces for their protection and facilitated oil exploration. British troops also occupied the ex-Italian colony of Libya and negotiations were proceeding, in 1946, to perpetuate the occupation of Cyrenaica as a UN Trust Territory. There were also British forces in Greece to prop up a government battling with communist insurgents.

As the Greek, Egyptian, Sudanese, Jordanian, Iranian and Iraqi troops marched down The Mall on 8 June, Britain held unprecedented sway in the Middle East, from Tripoli to Tehran, and from Athens to Aden. Yet as these contingents saluted the King-Emperor, they could not know that Attlee was engaged in prolonged battle with the Chiefs of

Staff, sitting on the opposite side of the saluting base, over whether it was worth Britain's while to retain its responsibilities in such 'deficit areas'.[2]

The farthest peripheries of Empire lay in the Pacific Ocean, where Britain was the dominant power in the islands, in association with Australia and New Zealand. Britain's largest Pacific colony was Fiji, whose Governor was also High Commissioner for the Western Pacific. He exercised overall control through Resident Commissioners in the British Solomon Islands Protectorate, the Gilbert and Ellice Islands Colony, and the Anglo-French Condominium in the New Hebrides, and he was represented in the Kingdom of Tonga, a Protected State, by a British Agent. The High Commissioner was also Governor of Pitcairn, home of the *Bounty* mutineers' descendants and the Empire's smallest, most distant, dependency. Nauru, the phosphate island, was a joint Australian-British-New Zealand Trust Territory, administered by Australia, which also ruled Papua and the Trust Territory of New Guinea, including the Bismarck Archipelago. New Zealand ruled the Trust Territory of Western Samoa, and the Cook Islands and Niue were treated as a part of New Zealand territory and were soon to be joined by Tokelau. Last of all, a large portion of the Antarctic continent was claimed for the Empire through the instrumentality of New Zealand's Ross Dependency, the Australian Antarctic Territory and the British Falkland Islands Dependencies.

Such was the size and span of the British Empire, a little more than three hundred years after the first settlements had been planted in Newfoundland and the West Indies. Having survived two world wars with its properties enlarged, the Imperial structure on display during the Victory Parade contributed significantly to Britain's feeling of self-congratulation. After the marching columns had passed the saluting base, there was a fly-past by three hundred war planes. The day ended in the 'Heart of the Empire' with floodlighting, fireworks, and neighbourhood festivities, while around the globe, from Canadian prairies to Pacific atolls, from teeming Calcutta to empty Antarctica, it could be said (in the words of a cliché of the time) 'the Empire still stands'.

The Meaning of Decolonization

That Saturday offered a brief and glorious moment of euphoria. Less than two years later, India, Pakistan, Burma and Ceylon were all independent and Palestine had become the State of Israel. Ten years on, Sudan gained independence and, in the Suez crisis of 1956, Britain experienced humiliating failure with moral support only from Australia and New Zealand. In the following year, the Gold Coast (Ghana) and Malaya became independent. A further ten years along – the 'Wind of Change' having swept over most of Africa – twenty-four more colonies had achieved independence. The creation of the Commonwealth Secretariat in 1965 removed the co-ordination of Commonwealth meetings and consultation from the corridors of Whitehall. Just two decades from the proud celebrations of 1946, decolonization was far advanced. In all the large dependencies, bar Palestine, power had been transferred by negotiation. Then in one, Southern Rhodesia, the minority settler regime seized power by making its own unilateral declaration of independence, UDI, in 1965.

By any yardstick, these were momentous events for British and global history. Yet they were so swift, and are so recent, that they remain subject to intense debate as to their sequence, motivation, impact and meaning. There is even disagreement as to the appropriate nomenclature? What does decolonization mean? How do we describe the fall of the British Empire?

'Counter-colonization and decolonization' were words adopted by Moritz Julius Bonn of the LSE in the 1930s.[3] 'Decolonization' only came into general currency at the end of the 1950s. The verb form, 'decolonize', is often given a one-way meaning, as if concerning action by only one party: 'to grant independence to a colony'[4] or 'to withdraw from a colony leaving it independent'.[5] But decolonization is more correctly defined in two dimensions: 'The withdrawal from its former colonies of a colonial power; the acquisition of political and economic independence by such colonies'.[6] Leopold Senghor defined it in intellectual terms much more broadly as 'the abolition of all prejudice, of all superiority complex, in the mind of the colonizer, and also all inferiority complex in the mind of the colonized'. Other definitions have it as a process in the context of international relations. Thus John Hargreaves interprets it as 'the intention to terminate formal political control over specific colonial territories, and to replace it by some new relationship'.[7] In similar, but more pointed, vein, Ronald Robinson and John Gallagher have suggested that nationalism, a prime instrument in the process, has been 'the continuation of imperialism by other means'.[8] In such a view, the moment of transfer of power is less significant than continuities of political and economic relationships. Prosser Gifford and Roger Louis see it as 'a process, not an event'.[9] Louis and Robinson, tracing the Cold War context of decolonization, have explored the paradox of the 'Imperialism of Decolonization'.[10]

In the light of such hints of continuity, what, then, did decolonization signify? Did the British Empire fall? The process whereby more than fifty British dependencies became independent states in the international community has been labelled with varying degrees of blandness. 'Imperialism' is a well-established label, but 'disimperialism'[11] is rarely used, 'decolonization' being the preferred word. 'End-of-Empire' is the simplest usage, 'Transfer of Power', 'Demission of Power', 'Empire-unbuilding' or 'Devolution' perhaps the most benign. 'Eclipse', 'Dissolution', 'Unscrambling', 'Crumbling', 'Collapse', 'Liquidation', 'Relinquishment' are all more vivid.[12] John Gallagher preferred 'Decline, Revival and Fall' and 'fall' is the chosen word for this work as it fits best with the contemporary mood of the British, if not their rhetoric.[13]

Those British ministers and officials responsible for doing the 'decolonizing' largely failed in what they thought they were about. Their search for unified, viable units was usually in vain. Their timetables were always overtaken by events. There was a real feeling of disillusionment and disintegration in the 1960s – almost one of a desperate race against time. It is true that the Commonwealth survived (indeed later revived), but it was not the 'British Commonwealth of Nations' so cherished by the close-knit, co-operating, élite membership up until the 1940s. By 1960 it was accepted with great reluctance, that, if a single mini-state with a half-million population was accepted as an equal member, 'all the other tiddlers' would demand the same. And, of course, they did. Decolonization never turned out as the British hoped and planned. Events usually achieved their own momentum.

The theme to be pursued is a narrow one – the gaining and granting of independence. This book is not about the relative decline of the British economy, or about Britain's endeavour to remain a world power, nor about post-imperial British society. The approach is largely political and constitutional, one which once dominated imperial studies but which has been increasingly discarded over the past thirty years. It is resurrected here because that is what the great debates of 1946–8 and 1960–3 were about. To whom should power be transferred? This involved wrangling about franchises, seats in legislatures, the shape of executive councils or ministries, the nature of constitutions. They were quite narrow, repetitive debates and the British were reluctant to move in the short run. Yet they always gave way and colonial status was ended, as had been long expected.

The Empire indeed 'fell'. But virtue was always made of necessity. Constitutional upheaval at home was avoided and the modern Commonwealth – the antithesis of Empire – survives.

Part I

WHEN DID THE BRITISH EMPIRE FALL?

The 'when' question is the easiest one to tackle. Everyone knows that the Empire fell soon after the 1939–45 war. From the partition of the Indian subcontinent into India and Pakistan in 1947, to the independence of Vanuatu and Zimbabwe in 1980, was a mere thirty-three years, half a lifetime. Some commentators adjust their focus much more sharply. John Darwin's stimulating and comprehensive account of British de-colonization stresses 'two great convulsive movements' in Asia, 1947–8, and Africa, 1960–4, and he reminds us that the outcomes on both occasions were unexpected and unwelcome in Britain.[1] Roger Louis is more specific and attributes it to decisions by the Attlee Government in 1947–8, and the Macmillan Government, 1959–61.[2] Others blur the focus and describe a more gradual and spasmodic process. John Gallagher traced his 'Decline, Revival, and Fall' back to the aftermath of the 1914–18 war. He stressed the revival of imperialism in the 1940s, but was conscious of 'small sparks eating their way through long histori-cal fuses'. For him the 1950s and 1960s were the age when imperialism ended, when 'at last, without convulsion, without tremor and without agony, the great ship goes down'[3] – but he was unspecific about the precise date. Dennis Austin, seeking the 'point of no return', wrote that whenever he was tempted to alight at a landmark, he found himself looking back to earlier way-stations on the road.[4]

To help clarify the question of sequence we may, initially, divide the broad sweep of British decolonization into six phases, which were uneven in pace and span. First, Dominion status, evolving in the nine-teenth century and reaching fulfilment in the Statute of Westminster of 1931, provided, for a time, a satisfying and powerful model and, briefly, a convenient procedural tool. Secondly, during 1947–8, the Attlee Government gave independence to India, Pakistan, Burma and Ceylon,

11

ended the Palestine Mandate and planned the end of Indirect Rule in African territories, such as Nigeria and the Gold Coast. Thirdly, in the ambiguous 1950s, the Churchill and Eden Governments tried to slow the process down. But they went ahead with short-lived federations in Central Africa and the West Indies, agreed to independence for Sudan, Ghana and Malaya, and even considered integrating Malta into Britain. Fourthly, Macmillan's 'Wind of Change', 1957–63, pushed nine African territories along the path to independence and permitted Cyprus to set the precedent for the smaller territories. Fifthly, Wilson's 'Withdrawal from East-of-Suez' after 1967 set in motion the abandonment of Aden and the Gulf States and the withdrawal of British forces from the Far East except for small garrisons in Hong Kong and Brunei. Finally, in the 1970s and 1980s the flag was lowered and the files closed on the Pacific Islands, the smaller Caribbean islands and Zimbabwe, leaving only some isolated islands and problem colonies like the Falkland Islands, Gibraltar and Hong Kong, whose futures depended on accommodation with their neighbours. In Hong Kong's case, the Sino-British Joint Declaration of 1985 provided for reversion to Chinese sovereignty as a Special Administrative Region on the expiry of the New Territories lease at the end of June 1997.

At this point, five hundred years after Cabot's first voyage from Bristol to North America, and fifty years after the ending of the Raj, a terminus was reached. To determine the critical points in these phases, each must be examined in turn.

1

THE DOMINION MODEL

The Dominion model, as defined in the Balfour Report of 1926, and given authority (almost sanctity) by the Statute of Westminster of 1931, was not designed as the first stage in the dissolution of Empire. It signified the evolutionary process whereby membership became equal and voluntary so that close co-operation, allegiance and influence could exist among independent states. In the 1939–45 war, all but one of the Dominions, acting independently, contributed to the war effort (some out of all proportion to their size), then joined the United Nations (UN) and their continued association lent some plausibility to Britain's efforts to remain as a great power. But, in contrast to the brief post-war decades of decolonization, Dominion status (which was ironically soon to be mysteriously discarded) had evolved over a century by a process of uneven incremental reform.

The label 'Dominion' (so Attlee told Nehru in 1948) was taken from the Bible and applied to the Canadian Confederation in 1867.[1] It was adopted at the 1907 Colonial Conference as a way of describing the group of self-governing colonies in North America, Australasia and Southern Africa. From various suggestions such as 'self-governing Colonies', or 'self-governing communities of the Empire', the label chosen was 'self-governing Dominions beyond the seas' – abbreviated in normal usage to 'Dominions'. But a more precise description, offered by Alfred Deakin, the Australian prime minister, was worded 'British Dominions possessing responsible government'.[2] This highlighted the particular system of self-government which was the defining characteristic of the Dominions and the vital element in their lengthy path to independence.

Responsible government had evolved between the 1820s and 1850s as a solution to inherent strains in the form of representative government

13

which had been inherited from the seventeenth-century colonies of the British Atlantic world. From earliest days, the colonies had been ruled by a Governor, advised by a council, who made laws through some form of assembly in which elements of the settler population were given a voice. In the late eighteenth century, in the aftermath of the American Revolution, the system was regularized in the remaining North American colonies by a deliberate mirroring of British constitutional practice in the shape of four institutions – the Governor (representing the Crown), an executive council (made up of officials who held the main government offices), a legislative council (or upper house of the legislature, made up of prominent citizens by appointment) and an elected assembly (to represent the colonists).[3] The institutions of individual colonies varied in their origins and nomenclature, but the principle became general and the system created inevitable conflicts. These were gradually diagnosed as a tendency to clashes between executive and legislature.

The Governor was responsible to the Crown, which in practice meant the British ministry which advised the Crown. But Governors, as temporary sojourners, were often not expert in colonial affairs or personalities. The assemblies were answerable to their electors and increasingly copied the Westminster parliamentary model, and sought to mimic the House of Commons as they demanded reforms in colonial government, especially control of money. The 'middle' element of the constitutions, the officials of the executive councils and the notables of the legislative councils, constituted close-knit ruling groups who appeared to be only responsible to themselves. It was realized in the Colonial Office by the 1820s that colonial legislatures understood their affairs better than London and that Governors would have to secure their co-operation. In 1828, James Stephen envisaged a Governor as 'Agent and Minister of the Assembly, rather than a co-ordinate or superior authority'.[4] Links between executive and legislature were sought, so assemblymen were occasionally appointed to executive councils and officials sat in assemblies. In 1837 Joseph Howe, a Nova Scotian politician, called for the 'blessings of the British Constitution', whereby ministers could not retain office if they lost the confidence of the parliamentary majority. Howe wanted enough assemblymen appointed to the council to ensure its 'responsibility to the Commons'.[5] In New Brunswick, a move was made in this direction when the assembly agreed in 1837 to grant a civil list to defray government expenses in return for gaining control over Crown lands and land revenue and the Governor was instructed by the Colonial Office to appoint an executive council so it would command the 'entire confidence' of the assembly.

This trend towards making the executive responsible to the legislature was highlighted (but also delayed) by minor rebellions of Upper and Lower Canada in 1837. They were easily suppressed by force, but Lord Durham's short-lived mission to North America in 1838 led to his celebrated Report of 1839, which provided eloquent endorsement of the trends for bringing harmony between executive and legislature which were already in train. Describing the old constitution as 'this system of irresponsible government', Durham prescribed what Howe and others were asking for, and New Brunswick already had. Here, government had been taken out of the hands of those who could not command a majority in the assembly and given to those who could. Said Durham: 'It needs but to follow out consistently the principles of the British constitution ... But the Crown must ... submit to the necessary consequences of representative institutions; and if it has to carry out the Government in unison with a representative body, it must consent to carry it on by means of those in whom that representative body has confidence.'[6] But Durham did not advocate the end of empire; he also wanted to define the boundaries of imperial and colonial authority and suggested reserving for the Crown power over the constitution, land, commercial laws and foreign affairs.

In the wake of the Canadian rebellions, the Durham prescriptions were not immediately acceptable. But in 1846, the Governor of Nova Scotia was instructed to select his ministers according to 'the wishes of the people themselves'.[7] After an election in 1847, Nova Scotia received the first fully responsible ministry in the Empire – a century before India's independence. The Canadas (now a single United Province) followed in 1848. The system was extended to the Australian colonies and New Zealand in the 1850s and to the Cape Colony in 1872, by which time English-educated reformers were already calling for the same system for India. The colonies became self-governing in internal affairs. The Crown acted in such matters on the advice of ministers, as in Britain. It was a system of government by leaders of the parliamentary majority, a system of ministerial rule.

Before the label 'Dominion' was adopted to distinguish these colonies, three developments occurred which accentuated their growing autonomy. First, two groups of colonies federated together to create very large geographical and political units. In 1867, the United Province of Canada split again into Ontario and Quebec and joined Nova Scotia and New Brunswick in the 'Dominion of Canada'. Manitoba joined in

1870, British Columbia in 1871, and Prince Edward Island in 1873, thus forming the largest single British territorial dependency. In 1901, the six colonies in Australia came together to form the 'Commonwealth of Australia', which was proclaimed as a 'continent for a nation and a nation for a continent'. (Four of the Southern African colonies would form the 'Union of South Africa' in 1910.)

Secondly, in the face of arguments about the line between imperial and colonial authority, especially in the matter of foreign affairs and defence (which became increasingly urgent because of rivalry with France and Germany), a series of consultative conferences involving Britain and the self-governing colonies were held in London. The first Colonial Conference was held in 1887, to coincide with Queen Victoria's Golden Jubilee. Others followed on royal galas such as the Diamond Jubilee of 1897, and the Coronation of Edward VII in 1902. By this time, the meetings had narrowed to become intimate gatherings of only the prime ministers of Australia, Britain, Canada, Cape Colony, Natal, Newfoundland and New Zealand, who were joined in 1907 by the prime ministers of the Transvaal and the Orange Free State. (After 1910 there was a single South African prime minister.)

The third development was the gradual whittling away of the imperial reserve powers. Land was soon handed over, as were changes to colonial constitutions and even commercial laws involving tariffs which conflicted with the imperial orthodoxy of free trade. Where disputes cropped up, and the Colonial Office was appealed to for a ruling, it invariably decided in favour of the principle of self-government over the technicalities of imperial sovereignty. Governors were told to act on the advice of their ministers. By the time of the 1907 conference, the chief practical reservation was confined to foreign affairs and defence.

By this time, too, the very word 'Empire' had begun to grate and the friendlier 'Commonwealth' was felt by Sir Henry Campbell-Bannerman to be a more 'homely, native phrase'. A description of the Empire as a community or family of countries made its first appearance in fugitive usages in the 1860s and 1870s, and featured in a much-quoted speech of Lord Rosebery in Adelaide in 1884, when he referred to the Empire as a 'commonwealth of nations'. Expanded to 'British Commonwealth of Nations', the new style was popularized during the 1914–18 war by Alfred Zimmern, Lionel Curtis and Jan Smuts. Close co-operation between the Dominions and Britain on numerous battlefields led to consultation in Imperial War Conferences and Imperial War Cabinets. In a conference resolution of 1917, the Dominions were referred to as 'autonomous nations of an Imperial Commonwealth'.[8] Smuts wanted to secure a definition of Dominion status after the war, but a dynamic new dimension was added when Southern Ireland received a form of Home Rule by treaty in 1921, whereby, as the Irish Free State, it was offered the same constitutional status in the 'Community of Nations known as the British Empire' as Canada, Australia, New Zealand and South Africa. In its own constitution, the Irish Free State (*Saorstat Eireann*) was described as 'a co-equal member of the community called the British Commonwealth of Nations'. Not all Irish nationalists approved. Republicans opposed the treaty and took up arms against the Free State Government for two years. Eamon de Valera proposed an alternative status in 1922, whereby Ireland would be an 'associate' of the Commonwealth, and for the purposes of the Association, would recognize the King as head of the Association.[9] But the Irish Government believed that it could advance the practice of Dominion status to the point when a republican Ireland, which might incorporate the northern counties, would become possible.

Dominion status also acquired other symbols of autonomy in the post-war years. The Dominions were separately represented at the Versailles Peace Conference in 1919, and they joined the League of Nations in their own right. In 1923, it was accepted that separate treaties might be signed with foreign countries. Soon, separate diplomatic missions were opened at the League of Nations and in Washington, led by the Irish, the Canadians and the South Africans.

To iron out remaining anomalies and some technicalities of sub-ordination and to avoid the occasional awkwardnesses which could arise from them, the 1926 Imperial Conference appointed a Committee on Inter-Imperial relations chaired by former prime minister, Lord Balfour. The formula contained in the committee's report, known as the 'Balfour definition', or 'status formula', comprised one succinct sentence (put in italic by the printer) which is clear and simple but also nicely ambiguous. Describing the mutual relations between Britain and the Dominions it runs: 'They are autonomous communities, within the British Empire, equal in status, in no way subordinate one to another in any aspect of their domestic or external affairs, though united by a common allegiance to the Crown, and freely associated as members of the British Commonwealth of Nations.' The Dominions were still *within the Empire*, but now voluntarily associated as *equal members of the Commonwealth*, all owing allegiance to the Crown. The key doctrine was *equality*, which became the foundation principle of the Commonwealth. But the report went on to say that 'the principles of equality and similarity appropriate to *status* do not universally extend to function'. In matters of diplomacy and defence 'flexible machinery' was also required.[10] The Balfour formula implied, then, that while Britain and the Dominions were equal in political status and would so treat each other in their round-table discussions, their very marked inequalities and differences in size, population, resources and military might would require pragmatic methods of co-operation in the international arena. It was also noted that there were certain areas of legal subordination which contradicted the principle of equality and required expert consideration.

This was provided in the conference on the Operation of Dominion Legislation which met in 1929 and identified five areas of legislative disability: the royal power of disallow or reserve colonial bills; limits to the extra-territorial jurisdiction of Dominion parliaments; the doctrine of legislative repugnancy as defined in the Colonial Laws Validity Act of 1865; and the two areas of maritime law contained in the Admiralty Courts and Merchant Shipping Acts. To remove these disabilities, a substantive enactment by the British Parliament was recommended.

This was provided in the Statute of Westminster of 1931, which gave legal sanction to the doctrines of equality, autonomy, common allegiance and free association. Sections Two to Six of the Statute eliminated the problems highlighted in the 1929 report. Section Four of the Act meant a renunciation of British power over the Dominions: 'No Act of Parliament of the United Kingdom passed after the commencement of this Act shall extend, or be deemed to extend, to a Dominion as part of the law of that Dominion, unless it is expressly declared in that Act that the Dominion has requested, and consented to, the enactment thereof.'[11] However, all had not been plain sailing in the drafting of the Act. The constitutions of Australia, Canada and New Zealand were Acts of the British Parliament and most of the Canadian Provincial and Australian State constitutions stemmed from imperial instruments. Therefore the Statute of Westminster did not apply to these. The New Zealand Government was, in fact, so content with the *status quo* and unhappy about being named in the statute that it only agreed to inclusion after the insertion of Section Ten, which provided that the operative sections Two to Six, would not apply to New Zealand unless specifically adopted by the Dominion Parliament. Australia and Newfoundland were also included in this section. This meant that, although the Dominions were as independent as they wanted to be from 1931, the Statute only applied at that point to Canada, South Africa and the Irish Free State. Australia planned to adopt it, but did not do so until 1942, and New Zealand waited until 1947. Newfoundland never did. It abandoned Dominion status in 1933 and became a province of Canada in 1949.

Whether the Statute of Westminster allowed a right of secession from the Empire/Commonwealth was disputed. The convention of 'free association', recorded in the second recital of the preamble, would imply that such association could be ended. But the same recital recalled that member countries were 'united by a common allegiance to the Crown' and that it would accord with 'the established constitutional position' that changes to the succession and the Royal Title would require the assent of the British and Dominion parliaments. Professor A. B. Keith argued from this that no Dominion could secede by unilateral action; separation would require the concurrence of the British and Dominion parliaments. As against this view, Professor K. C. Wheare pointed to Section Two of the Statute, which confirmed the full legislative equality of Dominion parliaments.[12]

The Dominion which went furthest in asserting its independence was the Irish Free State. As well as leading the way in the appointing of ambassadors, the Irish sent well-prepared and influential delegations to argue for autonomy at the 1926 and 1930 Imperial Conferences. In 1931, the King's signature was obtained for an Irish treaty without recourse to the intermediary of a Whitehall department as the text was taken to Buckingham Palace in person by the Irish external affairs minister. With the accession to power in Dublin in 1932 of the ardent republican, de Valera, the British government was asked to recall the Governor-General. In his place de Valera nominated a nonentity who lived in a suburban house, undertook no public duties, and so the vice-regal function lapsed. The oath of allegiance was ended, as were appeals to the Privy Council. In 1936 de Valera took the opportunity of the British Government's preoccupation with the abdication crisis to make fundamental changes in the Irish Free State's position as a Dominion, but without making any direct challenge to Britain and the Empire/Commonwealth.

The Executive Authority (External Relations) Act, 1936, confined the role of the Crown in the Free State to diplomatic formalities only. It provided that:

so long as the Saorstat Eireann is associated with the following nations, that is to say Australia, Canada, Great Britain, New Zealand and South Africa, and so long as the King recognized by those nations as the symbol of their co-operation continues to act on behalf of those nations (acting on the advice of the several Governments thereof) for

the purposes of the appointment of diplomatic and consular representatives and the conclusion of international agreements, the King so
recognized may, and is hereby authorized to, act on behalf of Saorstat
Eireann for the like purposes as and when advised by the Executive
Council to do so.[13]

This move was taken a stage further at the end of 1937, when, after a
referendum, a republican constitution was adopted in which the Irish
Free State was described as a 'sovereign, independent, democratic
State', with Irish as its first language and a directly elected President as
head of state. The style 'Republic of Ireland' was tactfully avoided, since
Ulster remained in the United Kingdom. The British Government, for
its part, announced that the new constitution of the Irish Free State
would not affect its position and that, under the new designation, 'Eire
or Ireland', it would remain a member of the British Commonwealth.
The other Dominions indicated that they agreed to this. Eire continued
to be treated as a Dominion, though its position in the Commonwealth
was one of 'external association'. This was most clearly demonstrated by
its choice of neutrality in the 1939–45 war. But, as ever, anomalies
abounded. Although a German ambassador remained in this Dominion
throughout the war, the Irish Government, without compromising
neutrality, gave assurances it would not allow Ireland to be used as a
base for attacks on Britain. Tens of thousands of Irish from Eire served
in the British forces. Moreover the Irish authorities passed on information about German ship and submarine movements, allowed a rescue
tug to be stationed in Cobh harbour, and permitted hot pursuit over
Irish sea and air space. When Belfast was bombed in 1941, de Valera
ordered the Dublin fire brigade to rush across the border.

Eire demonstrated most clearly that Dominion status could amount
to sovereign independence, as did Canada and South Africa and,
eventually, Australia and New Zealand. Dominion status, therefore,
provided a powerful model of independence achieved by evolution and
agreement. Yet, although it was cited as a goal for the more advanced
dependencies in Asia, Africa and the Caribbean, and played a brief, and
quite vital role, in the decolonization of South Asia in the early post-war
years, it was increasingly deprecated in many quarters and in the 1950s
was quickly dropped.

2

THE ATTLEE GOVERNMENT'S
DECISIONS OF 1947–8

Attlee's great contribution to decolonization was the transfer of power in India and the latter's acceptance in the Commonwealth as a republic. His experience went back twenty years to his membership of the Simon Commission which visited India in 1928 and 1929. And during the war, in January 1942, on the eve of the fall of Singapore, when a group of Indian elder statesmen called for a 'bold stroke [of] far-sighted states-manship' in the form of a national government for India with a con-stitutional position equal to the Dominions, Attlee, who had a history degree, called for a positive response. As he said to Churchill: 'Lord Durham saved Canada for the British Empire. We need a man to do in India what Durham did in Canada.'[1] Attlee believed India to be a candidate for routeing along the century-old track which led to the terminus of independence via Dominion status. However, India's experience was quite different from that of the settler colonies which became Dominions.

The Indian Empire, with its 400 million peoples, was the most populous dependency and in the Victorian hey-day was the biggest market in the Empire and took the largest portion of British imperial investment. Direct rule dated from 1858, when the Crown took over from the East India Company, but about a third of the sub-continent's land mass was made up of more than 600 Princely States, which were under British advice and protection. The Supreme Government at the centre was the Governor-General-in-Council and from 1877, when Queen Victoria became Empress of India, the imperial representative was styled 'Viceroy'. Governors presided over eleven provinces and in more than 200 districts the administrators of the Indian Civil Service were an élite of

21

about a thousand members, to which some Indians were recruited from 1870. With the inclusion of a small representative element from 1861, and some elected members from 1892, the structure of Indian councils began to resemble those in the colonies and political reformers, such as the members of the Indian National Congress, founded in 1885, called for responsible government as in Canada and Australia. By the early years of the twentieth century, the same crisis of relations between executive and legislature as had been experienced in North America eighty years earlier became evident in some provinces, notably Bengal.

To mark India's central position in the whole imperial structure, representatives of India were called to the Imperial Conferences from 1911; India was represented at the Versailles Peace Conference in 1919, and joined the League of Nations. In this way India's external status ran ahead of its domestic constitutional evolution, which was increasingly bedevilled by communal tensions. While 75 per cent of the population was Hindu, the 20 per cent Muslim minority included some Muslim majority regions. And as Hindus had responded first to English education and become prominent in the professions and the representative councils, Muslims began to demand separate representation, which was granted in 1909.

British responses to Indian political demands always came as too-little, too-late. The announcement of the goal of responsible government, in 1917, was accompanied by no timetable. The first instalment, called 'dyarchy', which began in 1921, provided for only half the governments in the provinces to be handed over to responsible ministers. This did not satisfy Indian nationalists, now led by M. K. Gandhi, who mobilized supporters to commit mass civil disobedience which, briefly, worried the government. In the wake of the Balfour definition of 1926, Indian moderates called for Dominion status, but radicals now wanted 'complete national independence' and to pre-empt them the Viceroy persuaded the British Government to announce, in 1929, that Dominion status would be the outcome of the 1917 promise. Again no deadline was stated. So once more, in 1930, Gandhi led another mass civil disobedience campaign. At the Round Table Conference held in London in 1931 the British conceded what Indian moderates wanted – a goal of responsible government at the centre for a future all-India federation made up of the provinces and the Princely States. But agreement could not be reached about the basis for representation. Gandhi and the Congress wanted the abolition of communal seats in legislatures; the Muslims and other minorities argued for their retention, which the British eventually confirmed.

From the Round Table Conference until the passage, in 1935, of the Government of India Act, which laid down a procedure for reaching Dominion status, the most critical debate about British decolonization took place. There were lengthy hearings by a parliamentary select committee. Conservative die-hards resisted reform every inch of the way, even taking it to division at the Conservative Party conference in 1933. The Act was the longest yet passed by the British Parliament and the debate took up five volumes of Hansard. This was agonizing on a scale which the British political élite would never again want to engage in, and thus it set the scene for the eventual ending of empire. In the Indian provinces responsible government was conceded and there was provision that when two-thirds of the Princely States had acceded to the federation, the centre would receive responsible government and the implication was that the new Indian Union would receive Dominion status. It was a recognition that the Raj would end. In the meantime, Indian ministries took office in the provinces after elections in 1937. However, the Union did not eventuate before the outbreak of the 1939–45 war, when the Viceroy's declaration that India was at war antagonized Indian leaders. As a result, Congress governments in seven provinces promptly resigned. Muslim-led governments stayed in office in four provinces and, in 1940, the All-India Muslim League (which had fared very badly in the 1937 elections) declared its goal of a separate Muslim state or states.[2]

Churchill, who had been leader of the die-hards in the 1930s, became prime minister in May 1940, and was inclined to put Indian reform on hold in the interests of winning the war, since India was a major base and source of troops. But L. S. Amery, the Secretary of State for India, like Attlee, favoured the Lord Durham prescription. In February 1942, he wanted to reaffirm the offer of Dominion status and he even told his Cabinet colleagues that they should also announce that a Dominion could secede from the Empire. In the event, Sir Stafford Cripps was sent to India in March–April 1942 to seek wartime co-operation from the Indian party leaders in return for promises of an Indian Union as a Dominion, with the possibility of some parts not joining but constituting another state, and the future constitution to be produced by an elected constituent assembly after the war. In a broadcast from New Delhi, Cripps told the Indians that they would be as free in every respect as Britain and the other Dominions.

The Cripps offer was rejected by Congress because it wanted the Viceroy's executive council to become a responsible cabinet immediately, and the Viceroy to behave as a constitutional monarch. But

Cripps said the British Government would not hand over power to a group of leaders who were not answerable to an elected legislature. Congress responded with the 'Quit India' movement, which turned into a violent revolt in August 1942, when considerable damage was done to government property and the railways. The movement was duly suppressed by force and the Congress leaders jailed for the rest of the war.

In spite of the impasse, the idea of Dominion status as a solution for India was not dead. In March 1943, President Roosevelt's representative in India told people he could not conceive of a country with more freedom than Canada. Amery prodded Churchill into allowing a further attempt at agreement. Amery wanted to hand over to an Indian transitional government and treat this as a Dominion government. The Viceroy, Lord Wavell, met the party leaders in July 1945, but Congress insisted on a united India, and Mohammed Ali Jinnah, the Muslim leader, said the creation of a Muslim Pakistan would be inconsistent with this.

The post-war Labour Government's first move was to call elections in India at the end of 1945. The results were clear: Congress won power in eight provinces; the Muslim League won most of the Muslim seats. Secondly, to avert Pakistan separation, the Cabinet mission visited India from March to May 1946. Cripps was the key figure in the delegation and produced the three-tier plan for an All-India Union, responsible for external affairs, defence, communications and minorities; groups of provinces and states as possible federations of 'Hindustan' and 'Pakistan' with delegated powers, and the provinces and states retaining residual powers. While the mission was still in India, Amery's idea of Dominion status was revived as a 'personal suggestion' by Sudhir Ghosh, a young Hindu, who had associated with Quakers at Cambridge, and who worked as a go-between for Gandhi. Ghosh advocated an interim central government, with equal numbers from Congress and the Muslim League in the Executive Council, which should be treated as a Dominion government.[3]

The Cabinet mission also suggested to Attlee that, if an interim government could be achieved, it should be treated 'as much like a Dominion Government as possible'.[4] Attlee, for his part, told the delegates to make it clear that India could be independent either inside or outside the Commonwealth. Although the Indian leaders rejected the Cabinet mission plan, the Viceroy went ahead with the idea of creating an interim government to take office until new arrangements could be formulated by an elected constituent assembly. Jawaharlal Nehru, as leader of the largest party (Congress) was asked to form a ministry. He appealed to Jinnah to take part, but Jinnah insisted that half the members should be Muslim and he then called for 'Direct Action' to achieve Pakistan. Nehru took office as vice-president of the executive council on 2 September 1946, and thus became a *de facto* 'premier'. In December he, Jinnah and Wavell went to London where appeals were made (even by the King) to persuade them to compromise. Wavell was pessimistic that British rule could be sustained for much longer and suggested setting a deadline for withdrawal.

It became apparent at the end of 1946 and in early 1947 that a vital watershed had been reached. Nehru and Jinnah could not agree. The Muslim League boycotted the constituent assembly, where Nehru raised the stakes by announcing the goal of an 'independent sovereign republic' for India. The Cabinet's India and Burma Committee came to feel that events were pushing them towards accepting Pakistan and they agreed to Wavell's idea of setting a date for departure. But Attlee felt that war-weary Wavell was not the man to effect it. He looked, instead, to the dynamic Lord Louis Mountbatten, the forty-six-year-old cousin of the King, recently returned from being Supreme Allied Commander in Southeast Asia. As the Cabinet met on the last day of 1946, Attlee was conscious they were at a major landmark in the history of the Empire. He and his colleagues agreed with Nye Bevan, the radical socialist minister of health, who said they must get the credit for seizing the initiative. The transfer of power must be presented as the logical and final step in the evolution of self-government. Britain did not need to make excuses for itself.[5] But Ernest Bevin, the foreign secretary, who was desperately trying to hang on to Britain's position in the Middle East, was more pessimistic. Writing next day to Attlee, he said that they needed a Viceroy to uphold the Empire. If India went, Malaya, Ceylon and the Middle East would be lost. But Attlee saw himself a realist, not a defeatist. What, he asked, was the alternative?

On 20 February 1947, Attlee announced in the House of Commons that the deadline for the transfer of power would be not later than 1 June 1948. If the constituent assembly had not completed arrangements by which a body would emerge to whom power could be transferred, the British Government would hand over 'in such other way as may seem most reasonable'.[6] Before Mountbatten set out to wind up the Raj, Sudhir Ghosh, who came to London to work in India House, passed on a proposal emanating from the Congress boss, Vallabhbhai Patel, suggesting one way to expedite the transfer of power would be to adapt the 1935 Act, treat the constituent assembly as an interim central legislature, and grant immediate Dominion status. India could be treated as a Dominion, pending decisions about future relations with the Commonwealth. The Secretary of State for India suggested these proposals were 'interesting as a straw in the wind'.[7]

Mountbatten discussed the Dominion status idea with Wavell when he reached Delhi on 22 March 1947. He told his staff that, when he met the various Indian leaders, he would warn them to keep their supporters quiet; it would count against them if they made trouble. He would be watching for people to whom it might be possible to transfer power. He said that some version of Dominion status might facilitate departure before the June 1948 deadline. By the end of March 1947, he was inclining towards partition into Hindustan, Pakistan and the States (including dividing Bengal and the Punjab) with a central board to control certain subjects. Gandhi issued the interesting challenge that Jinnah should be called to lead the interim government. This would get the Muslim League into the executive council and Jinnah would then have to win over the Hindu majority by the force of his advocacy. Mountbatten was shocked by the 'unrelieved gloom'[8] he found in the British administration. He felt they needed to get out quickly before there was civil war. By mid-April he realized that Jinnah was determined on Pakistan and that Congress (except for Gandhi) was prepared to let him have it. The Viceroy felt the 'sheer logic of events' was becoming the deciding factor.[9]

Having decided on partition, Mountbatten turned to keeping India in the Commonwealth. By granting Dominion status as early as possible, this 'most important single problem' might be solved.[10] A way for doing this, which was known to be acceptable to the Congress leaders, was drawn up by V. P. Menon, the Viceroy's Reforms Commissioner, on 25 April 1947. Dominion status could be granted as an interim measure; if they waited till mid-1948 there might be turmoil. A transfer of power could simply be made to one or two Dominions, which could later write their new constitutions without the pressing time-limit. Mountbatten sent his chief-of-staff to London with Menon's memorandum, saying that if it worked there was a sporting chance of keeping India in the Commonwealth. 'This is the greatest opportunity ever offered to the Empire.'[11] He told his staff to prepare now for a transfer of power in 1947; that the prestige factor was of overriding importance.

The final outcome in India was rich in irony. Nehru accepted that Dominion status would allow for early independence, but said it had to be shown that it meant complete independence 'without offensive phraseology'. Sir Hartly Shawcross, the Attorney General, suggested

Dominion status 'stinks' for Indians. Mountbatten agreed it had 'unfortunate associations' and called for ideas for a looser Commonwealth relationship. At the same time, at home, Sir Norman Brook, the secretary to the Cabinet, also suggested to Attlee the need for an alternative to Dominion status. Canada and South Africa had reservations about being styled 'Dominions beyond the seas' in the Royal Title. Even New Zealand had dropped 'Dominion' from its title, when it joined the UN. Just as Dominion status was coming to the end of its usefulness for the Dominions, then, it was being recommended as the procedural device to ensure a quick, clean end to the Raj.[12] Attlee announced, on 3 June 1947, that power would be transferred to two successor states, the Dominions of India and Pakistan, and it would be left to their respective constituent assemblies to determine their relations with the Commonwealth. The flag came down in Karachi and New Delhi on 14/15 August 1947.

Just over four months later Burma became an independent republic outside the Commonwealth. The Burmese, sometimes dubbed the 'Irish of the East', were not able to use Dominion status to secure their ends as had the Indians and the Irish. However, during 1946 and 1947, Attlee's Cabinet, working through its India and Burma Committee, made many interesting connections during the policy-making process. Burma had been an Indian province in the nineteenth century and went through the same evolution as the Indian Empire until separation in 1937. Then, it received responsible government with powers reserved by the Governor over external affairs and the non-Burman hill peoples whose states, on the peripheries of Burma, made up about a third of the land. The first Burmese premier was invited to the 1937 Imperial Conference and, at this point, Burma was on the route to Dominion status, a goal which was specifically announced in November 1941, but to be granted after the war.

Some, however, found a faster, alternative route to independence. A group of radical students at the University of Rangoon led by Aung San, who took on the sobriquet *Thakins* (Burmese for 'master'), responded to Japanese overtures and created a Burma Independence Army, which assisted the Japanese invasion in 1942. In 1943 they were granted independence by Japan but, as the tide of war turned, Aung San swung his army round to the British. Although the Burma Government-in-Exile wanted on its return to try Aung San for treason, Attlee sent out a new Governor in 1946 with instructions to call Aung San to the executive council and consult it as if it were a Dominion government. Aung San went to London and, in a joint agreement of 27 January 1947, he and Attlee announced that there would be a Burma constituent assembly, which would nominate an interim legislature, and that, until independence was finalized, Burma would be treated as a *de facto* Dominion.

As the pace quickened in India in 1947, once Dominion status was accepted as a suitable device for accelerating independence, Aung San demanded no less for Burma. He, too, wanted a deadline set for the transfer of power; to get less than India would, he wrote to Attlee, 'neither be equitable nor in the fitness of things'.[13] The Burmese also followed the Indians in announcing the goal of a republic. After the 3 June 1947 announcement of independence for Dominions in India and Pakistan by August, Aung San again demanded the same. But, at this point, the Governor of Burma told him that a republic would have to be outside the Commonwealth. Governor Rance reported to London, 'we have now come to the parting of the ways'.[14] The Burmese wanted the same as the Indians but Dominion status for India and Pakistan was seen as an interim measure, which would keep them in the Commonwealth while they wrote their new constitutions – a process expected to take several years. The India and Burma Committee felt that Burmese motives were different and decided, on 21 June 1947, that if Burma was conceded Dominion status in August and then quit the Commonwealth by the end of the year, it would bring Dominion status into contempt. There were some who feared that if Burma went out of the Commonwealth, Ceylon and Malaya would follow and Malcolm Macdonald, the Governor-General of Malaya, when consulted, revived the Eire model of 1937, but the Cabinet was not persuaded.[15] When Burma became independent on 4 January 1948, it was as the Union of the Republic of Burma, outside the Commonwealth.

Only a month later, at midnight on 3 February 1948, Ceylon became independent as another Dominion in the Commonwealth. Although there was close coincidence in time with India, Pakistan and Burma, Ceylon trod a different path to freedom. It was a Crown colony, the first of the Colonial Office dependencies to achieve independence. The procedure, therefore, was quite separate.

Ceylon had long been one of the most prosperous colonies, as a major world producer of tea. It had been the first Crown colony to have representative institutions in the nineteenth century and, by the 1920s, had experienced those tensions between executive and legislature which might have invited the Durham solution. Instead, the visiting Commissioner in this case, Lord Donoughmore, recommended an interesting experiment for circumventing the Durham model. Executive and legislative functions were combined in 1931, in a single democratically elected State Council, which provided advice to the Governor through a board of ministers, the members of which were responsible through State Council executive committees. It was a form of indirect ministerial responsibility, not the normal Cabinet responsibility, and it provided such defraction of power that, by 1938, the Governor was recommending normal responsible government. This was promised, in 1941, for consideration after the war. It was not enough for Don Stephen Senanayake, the vice-chairman of the board of ministers, who made insistent demands for Dominion status. In 1944, the Ceylonese ministers produced their own draft constitution. Lord Soulbury, who was sent out to report in December 1944, agreed and reported that in the long run 'giving too much and too soon will prove to be wiser than giving too little and too late'.[16] But the Colonial Office was circumspect in its procedures and usages. Here was the first colonial territory out of more than fifty to approach independence. A new constitution providing for ministerial responsibility was granted by Order in Council in 1946. Dominion was not mentioned. Parliament made provision for 'fully responsible status within the British Commonwealth of Nations', but the secretary of state had to admit this would not differ from Dominion status. Senanayake was called upon to form a government and in the Ceylon Independence Act, of 10 December 1947, Ceylon was named as a Dominion at last.[17] The transfer of power was one of the smoothest of the whole Empire.

It also inspired a note of optimism in at least one Colonial Office official. H. T. Bourdillon wrote on 10 May 1948 that Ceylon gave a new impetus to the evolution of the colonial empire. 'Dominion status for coloured colonial peoples, however sincerely professed as an objective, remained a castle in the air. It has now come down to earth.' Previously 'there has always been comfortable stress on the word "ultimate"'. The time had come when 'we can no longer continue in ignorance of our own intentions'. They had to formulate the experiment they were conducting. It was a 'gigantic experiment', of leading peoples as rapidly as possible to self-government while endeavouring to maintain friendly links. He thought the evolving Commonwealth was 'the boldest stroke of political idealism which the world has yet witnessed, and on by far the grandest scale'.[18]

While Dominionhood for Ceylon is remembered as one of the most trouble-free transfers of power, events further east in Malaya were more problematical. The inauguration of the Federation of Malaya on 1 February 1948, three days before Ceylon's independence, marked a major reversal in British policy. Only eighteen weeks further on, and the outbreak of the communist insurrection in Malaya provided yet another example of the way events would determine the pace of change.[19]

Malaya was, with Ceylon and the Gold Coast, one of the bright jewels in the Colonial Office crown. In the 1920s it had emerged as the world's biggest single producer of tin and rubber, which left it, by the 1940s, as the Empire's best dollar earner. But British sovereignty was confined to the Straits Settlements – the islands of Penang and Singapore and the mainland enclave of Malacca, half-way between. In the Malay Peninsula there lay a quaint mixture of polities – the four Federated Malay States in the middle, which really constituted an administrative union rather than a federation – and the Unfederated Malay States, four to the north and one in the south. The population was divided between Malays and Chinese (roughly equal) with a significant Tamil minority. The system was ripe for unification and reform. Thus, while the Japanese overran Malaya and Borneo in 1941–2, and contemplated adding them to a greater Indonesia, a Malayan Planning Unit, set up in the Colonial Office in 1942, envisaged a new start after the war.

The idea was that, in place of the Crown Colony of the Straits Settlements and the nine Malay Protected States, there should be a Malayan Union in the peninsula made up of the States (with Penang and Malacca added) and a separate colony of Singapore. In late 1945 Sir Harold MacMichael toured Malaya and got the rulers' signatures on new treaties ceding to the Crown, for the first time, full power and jurisdiction. The Union plan also included equal citizenship for Chinese and Indians as well as Malays. It was to be the basis for eventual self-government in the Commonwealth, another future Dominion.

The result was quite unexpected. The rulers, who had politely signed the new treaties, soon, equally politely, protested. Malay opinion, led by the aristocracy, mobilized virtually overnight against this demeaning of the Malay States. When Sir Edward Gent, one of the architects of Malayan Union, arrived to become Governor on 31 March 1946, the rulers politely boycotted his installation. By May, the United Malays National Organization had come into being to combat the Union, and Gent changed his mind, within a month, about its feasibility. Although this abrupt about-turn dismayed the Colonial Office, Gent was supported by Malcolm Macdonald, who came out as Governor-General at this time and found Malay opinion solid against the Union. He and Gent met with UMNO leaders and produced an acceptable alternative, the Federation of Malaya, which included central executive and legislative councils, but retained the State governments. After the start of the new Federation on 1 February 1948, it was expected that there would be no question of independence for many years to come. Indeed, on 28 May 1948, a report in the Eastern Department of the Colonial Office suggested that there was no sign of any serious trouble brewing in Malaya.[20] Less than three weeks later three planters were shot and a twelve-year Emergency had begun!

The pressure of events could not be ignored. Although in April 1949 Attlee and his colleagues produced a directive for the Federal High Commissioner indicating that Britain had no intention of giving in to the communists, and that the aim was to guide the peoples of Malaya to self-government and this could not be jeopardized by premature withdrawal, plans adopted in 1950 to defeat the insurgents were slow to take effect. Thus in June 1950, Malcolm Macdonald addressed a conference of Governors in Southeast Asia and pointed out that the assumption they had been working on, that there would be a twenty-year transition period before the country was ready for independence, was due for revision. The UMNO leader now spoke of fifteen years. But Macdonald predicted that, over the next five to ten years, as new university students came home from study in Britain, Australia, and Singapore, the pace would have to quicken.[21] As well as defeating the communist rebels and safeguarding their investments, the British would need to foster political advance.

The most decisive and traumatic episode in the Attlee phase of decolonization was the abandonment of the Palestine Mandate on 14 May 1948. The new State of Israel had no interest in the Commonwealth and its very existence vitiated Britain's relations with the Arab states. It is true that Britain's imperial role in the Middle East still had another ten years (and in the Gulf, twenty) to run, but the withdrawal from Palestine was one of the few ignominious hasty exits.[22]

Britain's hold on the Middle East arose from late-Victorian strategy. Cyprus had been occupied in 1878 as a base and pledge of support to the Ottoman Empire against Russia, and Egypt was occupied in 1882 to protect the Suez Canal. When the Ottoman Caliph sided with Germany in the 1914–18 war, the British backed the Arab revolt against the Turks and sponsored successor states in the lands of the Ottoman Empire. Mandates under the League of Nations were granted to Britain over Palestine, Transjordan and Iraq. But, by the Balfour declaration of 1917, Britain had also pledged itself to facilitate 'a national home for the

Jewish people' in Palestine, provided it did not prejudice the rights of existing non-Jewish communities. It was a pledge which bedevilled the Mandate. How could trusteeship for the Palestinian people be reconciled with a Jewish national home? Proposals for a partition in the late 1930s came to nothing.

After 1945, the Jewish national home had to be seen in the context of the ghastly revelations about the Holocaust; the existence of thousands of refugees in Europe; the influence of international Zionism; and the suggestion of the American President, Harry Truman, that room should be found for 100,000 Jewish refugees in Palestine. The British leaders, however, believed that concessions to Zionists would antagonize the Arab world and jeopardize Britain's whole position in the Middle East and thus endanger the Suez Canal, the Gulf oilfields, and its Cold War strategy. In Colonial Office circles the Palestinian Arabs were regarded as indigenous people being displaced by Jewish settlers, not unlike the Africans and the white settlers of Kenya. The population totals at the end of the war were 560,000 Jews to 1,200,000 Arabs. British policy favoured a bi-national state such as had long existed in Canada and South Africa. But by early 1947, as such a solution faded in India, it also became increasingly unlikely in Palestine. The plan was to grant provincial autonomy to Jewish and Arab cantons, with a central administration and representative legislature, and to prepare Palestine for independence after a five-year trusteeship. But to Jews this implied a permanent Arab majority and their terrorist units fought on to under-mine the British administration. Yet, to give in to the minority Jewish community would mean forfeiting Arab goodwill in Palestine and throughout the whole region, so British troops tried to suppress the terrorists. In 1947, this became an increasingly thankless task, tying down 100,000 troops, a tenth of the military manpower of the entire Empire.

After discussions in London early in 1947 failed to achieve com-promise between Jewish and Arab representatives, the Government announced, on 18 February 1947, that the Palestine issue would be referred to the UN. As opinion there turned increasingly towards partition into separate Jewish and Arab states, the Attlee Government announced that British troops could not be used to enforce a solution neither community desired. On 26 September 1947 (just five weeks after the partition of India) the Cabinet set another deadline – Britain would withdraw from Palestine no later than 1 August 1948. When the UN voted in favour of partition on 29 November 1947, the British Government refused to implement it. It admitted failure in Palestine; the

Mandate had become unworkable. When they left at midnight on 14 May 1948, they did not transfer power to anyone. The State of Israel proclaimed its independence and immediately extended its borders by armed force. The Palestinians were left without a state and were ousted from their lands.

When India and Palestine were partitioned, the British Government refused to use its troops to prevent violence between the separating communities. In Malaya, by contrast, they did use force to hold, and eventually suppress, a communist insurgency. They also used force to prevent violence getting out of hand in the Gold Coast, where riots broke out in 28 February 1948, and where, again, there were fears of communist subversion. Thus, the Gold Coast riots of 1948 became yet another accelerant to political change, but here the Colonial Office sent out a strong Governor to grasp the initiative, apply lessons learnt in fighting the communists in Malaya, and this gained about five years respite for implementing policies which had been contemplated in less frenzied times.[23]

In the colonies of tropical Africa, where there had been long-standing contact with the coasts, the expansive inland boundaries drawn around watersheds and across deserts dated only from the scramble of the 1880s and 1890s. Little had been done to develop or even rule these lands. Territories were often enveloped, not for their resources, but to keep out rival powers. The prevailing doctrine was 'Indirect Rule'. Building on the precedents of the Indian Princely States, the Malay States and the chiefdoms of Fiji, African governors used indigenous rulers, either readily identifiable Emirs as in Northern Nigeria, or appointed 'warrant chiefs' who the British picked out in less easily understood regions. The rules for Nigeria were systematized (and bureaucratized) in political memoranda by Lord Lugard in the early years of the century. A slightly more modernizing version, dubbed 'Indirect Administration', was promulgated by Sir Donald Cameron in Tanganyika, and later Nigeria, between the wars. The system, wrote Cameron, was designed 'to adapt for the purposes of local government the tribal institutions which the native peoples have evolved for themselves, so that the latter may develop in a constitutional manner from their own past, guided and restrained by the traditions and sanctions which they have inherited, moulded or modified as they may be on the advice of British Officers . . .' Cameron wanted to identify carefully the 'authority which according to tribal tradition and usage has regulated the affairs of the tribal unit', but purge it of abuses and 'educate the Native Authorities in their duties as rulers of their people according to civilized standards'.[24] It was hoped that such Native Authorities would unite in regional federations which might become the basis of representation in provincial councils and central legislative councils as eventual steps to representative government.

Those representative institutions which did exist were confined to the coastal colonies, where a few Africans had been nominated to legislative councils in the nineteenth century, and elected members had been introduced in the 1920s. These political beginnings had become the focus of 'nationalist' ambitions among the tiny western-educated élite, such as the National Congress of British West Africa in the 1920s and the Youth Movements in the Gold Coast and Nigeria in the 1930s. In 1937, Margery Perham, an Oxford scholar, pointed to an 'incongruous dualism' of goal for Africans; the small educated élite spoke 'the complete language of British parliamentary democracy' in the legislative councils. She suggested diverting their energies to modernizing the Native Authorities.[25]

During the 1939–45 war, serious thought was given in the Colonial Office to the future of tropical Africa. Reforming governors like Sir Alan Burns, who went to the Gold Coast, called for Africans to be appointed to executive councils, for elected majorities in the legislative councils, and for Africanization of the civil service. These, he argued, would eventually be demanded and, in the meantime, the administration needed to win local supporters. In 1942, two Africans were appointed to each of the Gold Coast and Nigerian executive councils. Plans were also made for giving the legislative councils wider powers and elected majorities. But this amounted to tinkering appropriate to pre-war demands. The new look at Africa undertaken in the Colonial Office in the 1940s had three main features.

First, under the Colonial Development and Welfare Acts, funds were voted by Parliament for 'development', especially in economic infrastructure, new products and social and health services. There were even exaggerated dreams that developing the 'great estates' could help solve Britain's post-war shortages. Secondly, it was realized that Indirect Rule and the Native Authorities were a poor basis for such economic and social development. Instead, democratically elected local councils were to become the basis of modern local government. In this way, political development was to begin at the grass roots. Put cynically by one official, it could mean calling on the illiterate masses to counter the influence of élitist demagogues. On 25 February 1947, Arthur Creech Jones, the secretary of state, circularized Governors with his celebrated local government dispatch, which presaged the end of Indirect Rule. Thirdly, since development would require political collaborators, a gradual route to self-government was mooted in the Caine–Cohen–Robinson proposals of 22 May 1947 which, Ronald Robinson suggested, was a Durham report for Africa.[26]

Stemming from agenda preparations for a Governors' summer school, later in the year, one report by Sidney Caine accepted that while the *pace* of change was at present still under Colonial Office control, the *direction* could not be altered: 'we must assume that perhaps within a generation many of the principal territories of the Colonial Empire will have attained or be within sight of the goal of full responsibility for local affairs.' This ought to be achieved by substituting 'friendly association' in place of 'benevolent domination' and should lead to a relationship approaching that with the Dominions. Some of the larger territories might look forward, some day, to full Dominion status, but this was unlikely for many small colonies.[27]

A four-stage advance to self-government was envisaged by Andrew Cohen and Kenneth Robinson. First, a 'Member system' should be adopted, whereby branches of central government should be grouped under members of the executive council to create the 'foundation on which a full Cabinet system may ultimately be built'. The council might have members for finance, law, economic development, and social services. The Governor would retain final authority but, under his chairmanship, the council should go beyond a purely advisory role. Unofficial members would provide links between executive and legislative councils. Secondly, non-officials could be made members-in-charge of departments and these could be progressively increased in number so that the executive could 'become increasingly responsible to the Legislature'. Thirdly, the members would become ministers under 'a system of Cabinet responsibility'. The Governor would still retain responsibility for some matters but in others ministers would be responsible to the legislature as in 'dyarchy'. The final stage would be reached when all departments came under ministers and 'internal self-government could be granted'.[28] Adopting such a procedure would avoid a sudden leap to responsible government as in the old Dominions and Indian provinces, or even the half-leap of dyarchy. The same end would be reached by a process of gradual adjustment. Cohen suggested that in the Gold Coast, the most politically advanced colony, such internal self-government was unlikely to be achieved in 'much less than a generation'.

Such leisurely cogitations were rudely shaken by the Accra riots of February 1948. Reading the committee of enquiry's report, Cohen realized that the appointment of African ministers had become urgent.

An all-African commission was appointed to draft a new constitution. It recommended a system of dyarchy, with an elected majority in the legislative assembly. In the executive council three senior officials only should remain responsible to the Governor, while eight Ministers would be responsible to the assembly. Yet, while members of the pre-war élite were drafting this gradualist constitution, a radical nationalist leader recently returned from Britain, Kwame Nkrumah, had emerged to create the Convention Peoples Party and call for 'Positive Action'. The Colonial Office sent as Governor Sir Charles Arden-Clarke, fresh from Southeast Asia where he had learnt the tactics used in the Malayan Emergency. He strengthened the Gold Coast security forces, and, declaring a State of Emergency in January 1950, he arrested the CPP leaders for inciting disorder. The first general elections were held peaceably on 8 February 1951, with the CPP calling for 'Self-Government Now', but with Nkrumah behind bars. When it transpired that the CPP had won a clear majority of elected seats, the Governor faced a critical dilemma.

Arden-Clarke then made what Roland Oliver has called the 'Gamble for Africa'.[29] Releasing Nkrumah from jail on 12 February 1951, he summoned him to form a ministry and become 'Leader of Government Business' in the Assembly. Nkrumah immediately announced the goal of Dominion status for the Gold Coast, which sent shock-waves around the Commonwealth, not least in South Africa. A general review of the ultimate goals of self-government in colonial territories would follow. But Arden-Clarke had seized the initiative. He wanted to build Nkrumah up as a 'Prime Minister' and hoped that, with such a titular change, a breather might be gained before further advances. In the Colonial Office, Cohen realized that full responsible government needed to be approached gradually, that they should endeavour to keep the Gold Coast in the Commonwealth, and that they might be able to hold off change for three or four more years. His doubts, expressed four years earlier, about self-government being likely within a generation had been shattered. Events had taken over.

Nkrumah's precipitate insistence on the goal of Dominion status raised a problem which had already troubled Attlee and would alarm his successors. He had willingly accepted disengagement from South Asia and Palestine and only reluctantly acquiesced in retaining a great power role in the Middle East. But when it came to allowing independence to the many small colonies Attlee drew the line.

The Cabinet's Committee on Commonwealth Relations discussed a request from Gibraltar, on 26 July 1948, for an elected-majority legislative council in place of rule by Governor-in-Council. This fortress colony had evacuated over 16,000 of its civilians during the war, mainly to Britain. By 1948, they had nearly all returned, but Attlee doubted whether a population of 25,000, which already had a municipal council, really needed *two* representative bodies. Although the secretary of state for colonies won over his colleagues to fulfilling a promise which had been made to the Gibraltarians, Attlee said they ought to look into the constitutional future of small colonies. Thus a special committee of enquiry consisting of officials, MPs and two historians met over 1949–51 to consider the future of twenty-one of the smaller territories. It was assumed that *none* would become independent. Some might be considered for the Tonga model (of a treaty relationship) or even incorporation into the UK (like the Isle of Man), but all the committee could suggest for most of them was a new status of 'Island' or 'City State'.[30] It was only a month before the Attlee Government left office. The idea was deemed 'academic and un-English' and quietly buried in the files. In spite of its momentous decisions of 1947–8, Attlee's Government was not about to demolish the Empire.

3

THE AMBIGUOUS FIFTIES

When the Conservatives came to power under Winston Churchill following the 25 October 1951 elections, half a decade of ambiguity and agonizing about colonial policy ensued. The secretary of state for colonies, Oliver Lyttelton, started off by informing the House of Commons, on 14 November 1951, that the new government would continue the policy of 'helping the Colonial territories to attain self-government within the British Commonwealth'.[1] But Churchill remained a cautious imperialist. His world-view focused on three interlocking circles – the English-speaking peoples, Western Europe, and the Empire/Commonwealth – with Britain in the unique position of being the only participant in all three. His priorities were stated on 29 November 1951: 'Our first object is the unity and the consolidation of the British Commonwealths and what is left of the former British Empire. Our second, the "fraternal association" of the European-speaking world; and the third, United Europe, to which we are a separate closely – and specially – related friend and ally.'[2] In 1954 he was still dreaming of a worthy new Colonial Office building across Parliament Square in Westminster at the 'Heart of the Empire'.

The Conservative Government showed firmness in many directions. It sent a strong man, in General Templer, to finish off the communists in Malaya; it declared an emergency in Kenya in 1952 and put down the Mau Mau revolt; it dismissed the Marxist-inclined ministry of Cheddi Jagan in British Guiana where a new constitution was suspended after only five months in 1953; the Kabaka of Buganda was sent into exile from Uganda; Field Marshal Harding was sent to beat the EOKA terrorists in Cyprus, and the Commonwealth Far East Strategic Reserve was created in Malaya. The Government was always concerned to create large, economically viable units, which would enhance British influence. Thus the Federation of Rhodesia and Nyasaland was created on 1 August 1953, giving the white settlers of Central Africa enhanced autonomy in an effort to erect a middle Dominion in Africa as a counterpoise to South Africa. In the Caribbean, while ministerial government went ahead in Barbados, Trinidad, and Jamaica, independence could not be expected until the West Indies federated. A Permissive Bill was passed, on 2 August 1956, authorizing federation, but it did not come into effect for another two years. The Government also had hopes for an East African federation and a federation of Malaya and the North Borneo territories. In all these matters the Conservatives took a firm line. Yet the momentum of decolonization could not be reversed. Libya became the first new African state on 24 December 1951, with British and American base rights secured by treaty. Sudan, the largest British territory in Africa, became independent on 1 January 1956, as part of an abortive bid to maintain British influence in the Middle East. Decisions were also made in 1956 for independence in the Gold Coast and Malaya, which came to fruition in the following year.

The Gold Coast was the critical case because it re-opened the whole question of Dominion status, Commonwealth membership, and the future of the smaller colonies. Nkrumah's demand for Dominion status immediately caused debate as to whether full self-government was the same as equal membership of the Commonwealth, and officials began to toy with the idea of a 'limbo' status without full membership. By March 1952, Lyttelton had persuaded the Cabinet to accept Governor Arden-Clarke's idea of giving Nkrumah the title Prime Minister and making the executive council a Cabinet. It was to be a change of name rather than substance and was intended to stave off further advances for a few years. Churchill was concerned at the expected South African reaction to a black prime minister and wanted to put the blame on the Labour Government, but did not send the cable he had drafted. In June 1952, Lyttelton made it clear to Nkrumah that Dominion status was something which had to get the approval of all the full members of the Commonwealth. Meanwhile a group of official and ministerial committees studied the criteria for membership, which had also arisen as Sudan approached independence. In 1953, Lyttelton still hoped that some 'mezzanine status' could be devised.[3] Another official ventured the notion of 'independence minus' – a status with the advantages of autonomy without the obligations of Commonwealth co-operation.[4] An official committee in January 1954, chaired by Sir Norman Brook, the Cabinet Secretary, tried to predict the shape of the Commonwealth in ten to twenty years' time. Those countries which might expect full independence were Gold Coast, Nigeria, and the federations in Central Africa, the West Indies and Malaya–North Borneo. There were also four 'intermediate' territories – Kenya, Uganda, Tanganyika and Sierra Leone – which would follow. But there were twenty-three small colonies which were 'never likely to achieve full independence and cannot aspire to the status of full Commonwealth membership'. Brook was aware that the Gold Coast case marked 'a decisive turning-point in the evolution of the Commonwealth connection'; but in April 1954, Arden-Clarke reported that Nkrumah was 'emphatic' that he would not accept a lesser status. The Gold Coast would rather leave the Commonwealth, and that would mean the loss of the rest of Africa. Thus, the Commonwealth Secretary concluded, on 11 October 1954, that there was 'no practical alternative' to sponsoring the Gold Coast for full membership.[5] The Cabinet accepted this reluctantly, on 7 December 1954, but it was three years before independence was actually granted on 6 March 1957.

Although the Gold Coast, a comparatively prosperous, dollar-earning colony, was on Brook's list of likely Commonwealth members, alternative futures were still sought for the many small colonies. When, during the course of these discussions, the Government announced, on 28 July 1954, that it would attempt to restore a representative legislative council in Cyprus, Harry Hopkinson, the minister of state in the Colonial Office, was goaded by the Labour opposition into admitting that Cyprus would be in the non-member category. James Griffiths (a former colonial secretary) asked if Dominion status, with the right to secede, was envisaged for Cyprus. Hopkinson replied: 'it has always been understood and agreed that there are certain territories in the Commonwealth which, owing to their particular circumstances, can never expect to be fully independent'.[6] In the other Mediterranean case, Malta, the Government even entered negotiations in 1955 to integrate the islands into the UK, with Maltese members at Westminster and full participation in the welfare state. The plan was dropped after an indecisive referendum in January 1956. As an alternative to Dominion status, the official committee came up with the concept of 'Statehood', but when first offered to Singapore in 1956, it was rejected. The Singaporeans wanted Dominion status; the Colonial Office insisted on reserve powers over internal security and the constitution. But in 1959 Singapore, after new elections, did become a self-governing state.

If the Gold Coast was the test case for full Commonwealth membership, it was in Malaya where the British not only began to accelerate the pace, but also agreed to underwrite internal and external security. Templer's initial timetable for Malaya envisaged local body elections in 1954–5, federal elections in 1956–8, and creation of a national government around 1960. But the continuance of the communist threat and the success of the United Malays National Organization in local elections, in September 1953, convinced Templer that UMNO should be brought into the executive council. Tengku Abdul Rahman, the party leader, went to London in May 1954, and asked for some political progress lest extremists prevail and they were all overtaken by events. On 21 July 1954, the British Cabinet agreed to federal elections in the following year. After the overwhelming victory of the 'Alliance' of UMNO and Chinese and Indian parties on 30 July 1955, Tengku Abdul Rahman was called to be chief minister. He was envisaging independence in four years, in 1959. But, after abortive negotiations in December 1955, with the communist leader Chin Peng, who refused to abandon his revolutionary aims, UMNO delegates flew to London to negotiate future plans in January 1956. Asked by the Malays, 'Are you going to make things difficult for us?', Sir John Martin of the Colonial Office replied, 'No, we are going to give it to you on a golden platter.'[7] It was agreed that there would be an interim period before full self-government: this would be achieved in August 1957 after a constitutional commission had visited Malaya to report on state and federal institutions and the judiciary. The Colonial Office even thought ahead about Commonwealth membership and planned for consultation well before independence.

From Nkrumah's first election victory in February 1951 to Ghana's independence in March 1957 was six years; from the Tengku's victory in 1955 to 'Merdeka' in August 1957 was two years. Malcolm Macdonald's prediction about an accelerating pace was fully realized. Noel Hutten, parliamentary counsel to the Treasury, expressed the bewilderment of the Whitehall law drafters in June 1957.

I think we have never yet had to do so many contradictory things simultaneously. Within the last ten years we have seen a part of Her Majesty's dominions turned into a foreign country without frills (Burma); a part of these dominions converted into two separate Dominions, and subsequently recognized as independent Republics within the Commonwealth (India and Pakistan); a colony converted into a Dominion without frills (Ceylon); an association of a colony, a protectorate and a trust territory converted into a Dominion, in this case involving an element of annexation (Gold Coast); a colony and two protectorates federated without annexation (Rhodesia); and other operations in respect of Southern Ireland and Palestine. In the present case [Malaya] we are running together the operation of federating two colonies and nine protected states, ceding sovereignty over the colonies and jurisdiction over the States, and treating the end product simultaneously as an independent sovereign country and a self-governing Dominion.[8]

In this way, he expressed vividly the spirit of the ambiguous fifties.

After Churchill had retired in 1955, Anthony Eden tried one piece of decisive action at Suez in 1956 – the result was humiliation and the collapse of British prestige in the Middle East. Suez, in turn, made its mark on the decolonization process.

When the Conservatives had come to power in October 1951, they had inherited the aftermath of recent, unresolved assaults on Britain's two major assets in the Middle East, the Suez Canal and the Gulf oil-fields – physically symbolized by the Canal Zone military bases and the Abadan refinery of the Anglo-Iranian Oil Company. In May 1951, the government of Dr Mossadeq in Tehran had nationalized the oil company and the question arose as to whether Britain should use force to hold Abadan. The manager of the refinery said that if Abadan were lost, the Suez Canal would be lost in five years. On Attlee's insistence, restraint was shown at Abadan and on 4 October 1951 the refinery was evacuated.[9] Four days later, the Egyptian Government unilaterally denounced the 1899 Sudan Condominium Treaty and proclaimed King Farouk of Egypt as King of the Sudan, and it also denounced the 1936 Treaty governing British base rights in Egypt. British troops in the Canal Zone were increasingly harassed and reviled and, in January 1952, a clash between Egyptian police and British troops in Ismailia was followed by 'Black Saturday', 26 January, when Shepherd's Hotel, the Turf Club and other favourite haunts of the British in Cairo were torched by mobs.

In the Abadan case, patience and co-operation with the Americans led to the removal of Mossadeq by the Shah in 1953, and a new oil regime in Iran in which BP had a share. In Egypt new opportunities arose when King Farouk was deposed, later in 1952, by young officers who were willing to forgo Egypt's claims on the Sudan in the interest of removing the British. Thus independence for the Sudan became possible and began on 1 January 1956. After Colonel Gamal Abd al-Nasser came to power in Egypt in 1954, and stood forth as the champion of the Arabs against the imperialists, the British decided to quit the Suez base. By an agreement made in 1954, the Canal Zone was evacuated over an eighteen-month period, but rights to return in wartime were maintained. The last troops left on 18 June 1956, and Middle East HQ was transferred to Cyprus. But while this move, which was supposed to herald a new era of good relations, went ahead, it was learned that Egypt was receiving arms from the Soviet bloc via Czechoslovakia. The Americans, supported by the British, withdrew funding for a high dam at Aswan on the Nile. In reply, Nasser nationalized the Suez Canal on 26 July 1956 to pay for the dam.

During weeks of negotiations, led by the Americans, to get Nasser to 'disgorge'[10] and permit an international canal regime, Eden contemplated using force to re-occupy the canal and topple Nasser. His pretext was provided by the French. Paris was the home of the Suez Canal Company, and France and Israel devised a plan whereby Israel would advance towards the canal to give France an excuse for intervening to protect it. The French needed bases in Cyprus, so drew the British into a secret pact of 'collusion' made at Sèvres on 27 October 1956. Eden had other fears, for if, in the event of an Israeli–Egyptian war, Jordan, as a sympathetic Arab state, got involved and invoked the British–Jordanian defence agreement, Britain would be ranged against Israel.[11] Thus, the fateful plan was hatched. On 29 October 1956, Israel invaded Egypt but stopped short of the Canal. A Franco-British ultimatum to the belligerents was made on 30 October, and the following day Egyptian air bases were bombed. Landings at Port Said followed on 6 November, by which time a severe run on the pound and expressions of American anger had shaken Eden and the Cabinet. The UN called for a cease-fire and with their forward patrols only twenty-five miles from Suez, the invaders stopped.

Suez shattered Britain's prestige in the Middle East and, indeed, the world. It demonstrated that Britain could not succeed independently as a power (even alongside France) without US support. Suez also rocked the Commonwealth and breached conventions of consultation, which were never fully restored. The Asian members were alienated and Canada led the move in the UN for inserting a peace-keeping force. Diplomatic support was forthcoming only from Australia and New Zealand and, in the latter case, Suez provided a poignant watershed. The prime minister, Sid Holland, probably had popular backing when he offered fulsome support to Eden. He even allowed New Zealand's recently acquired cruiser, the *Royalist*, to join the British attack fleet and its crew went on alert on 30 October. But officials pointed out that New

Zealand could be charged with aggression in the UN, and the Cabinet began to get cold feet. Thus, in a cable of 1 November, redolent with imperial rhetoric and stress upon 'ties of blood and Empire', Holland admitted they did not relish the prospect of charges of aggression and did not want to jeopardize relations with the US, New Zealand's main protector.[12] It was suggested that the cruiser could stay with the fleet but not be used operationally. In the event, it sailed for home on 4 November. Whether it had had any part in the Suez operations remains a moot point. Holland, it seems, had some sort of stroke or heart attack on the day the news of the invasion came.

Similarly in London, Eden's health was shattered and he left for a holiday in Jamaica before withdrawals were completed. He resigned in January 1957, handing over to Harold Macmillan, who had told an American colleague that Britain would rather go down with colours flying than be reduced to the status of the Netherlands. Even so, as Chancellor of the Exchequer, he faced the American refusal to bail out the pound. As prime minister, Macmillan would concentrate at first on restoring relations with the US, but he would soon proclaim the 'Wind of Change' in Africa.

4

MACMILLAN AND THE 'WIND OF CHANGE', 1957–63

One of Harold Macmillan's first moves was to instruct the Cabinet's Colonial Policy Committee, on 28 January 1957, to do three things. First, it was to consider future constitutional developments and indicate which colonies would be ripe for independence in the near future. Secondly, it was to identify those which would qualify as full members of the Commonwealth and suggest an appropriate future for those which would not. Thirdly, he called for 'something like a profit and loss account' for each colony so that ministers would be aware what would be gained or lost by granting independence.[1] The resulting 76-page report suggested that the immediate candidates for independence were Malaya (already set for August 1957), Nigeria (in 1960 or 1961) and the Caribbean and Central African Federations. Rapid advance could also be expected in West and East Africa and fourteen territories could expect internal self-government over the next ten years. Most of the smaller territories, however, had no material value and could not hope to maintain themselves with stable administrations if the British left. Withdrawal from them would not achieve large savings and it would be 'a negation of responsibility and indeed be degrading' to abandon them.[2] A separate report on financial and economic issues concluded that benefits and liabilities were 'evenly matched' and that Britain's economic interests were 'unlikely in themselves to be decisive in determining whether or not a territory should become independent'. Premature withdrawal could cause instability and create a bewilderment which would be 'discreditable and dangerous'.[3]

Macmillan's celebrated profit and loss analysis, then, was inconclusive and did not prompt an immediate acceleration in decolonization.

Macmillan was primarily concerned, in the post-Suez years, to restore relations with the United States and recover influence and intimacy within the Commonwealth. To do this, he met President Eisenhower in Bermuda and made his eastern tour in 1957–8 to India, Singapore, Australia and New Zealand, his visit to Canada in 1958, and his famous 'Wind of Change' tour of Africa in 1959–60. Macmillan wanted to retain the initiative. When speaking to the annual conference of British representatives in the Far East and Pacific at Singapore on 19 February 1958, he said that, while Britain could not match the power of the US and the USSR, it 'still chose to remain a great Power'. He admitted that resources were stretched but 'though we no longer had authority, we still had great influence'. He said he certainly had 'no intention of presiding over the liquidation of the British Empire'.[4] The first colonial moves by his government did not break new ground. Ghana and Malaya duly had their independence days. Nigeria followed Ghana's example; it received self-government under a federal system with a prime minister appointed in 1957, and went on to independence in 1960. Singapore finally agreed to become a self-governing state (something less than a Dominion) in 1959. The Federation of the West Indies began on 23 February 1958, with the goal of independence by 1962. In Cyprus, where British lives were being lost fighting EOKA terrorists, Macmillan insisted on a negotiated settlement allowing independence. These moves were all an extension of pre-Suez evolution.

At the beginning of 1959, a conference of Governors discussed prospects in East Africa, where the white settlers dominated in Kenya. It was now admitted that the British territories could not be kept in 'perpetual colonial status'. But while African control could be envisaged in Tanganyika and Uganda, Lennox-Boyd, the colonial secretary, could not see any prospect in the foreseeable future of Britain relinquishing control of Kenya. Of the three options presented, retreat and withdrawal by 1965 would leave a dangerous vacuum, and holding on would not appeal to world opinion. This left only the course of 'gradualness', with the assumption that Tanganyika and Uganda might have elected ministries by about 1969.[5] When this was discussed at the Colonial Policy Committee on 17 April 1959, it was mooted that unofficial members might reach equality in the legislatures by 1961 and achieve majorities between 1965 and 1969. Macmillan, summing up this discussion, found the long-term future in Africa 'presented a sombre picture' but said they should opt for 'step by step constitutional advance'.[6] Within two months, his pessimism was sharply confirmed by two incidents which roused British public and parliamentary opinion and shook him personally.

In June 1959, reports about the Hola detention camp in Kenya, where eleven Mau Mau detainees had been beaten to death, gave rise to a passionate debate in the House of Commons. In the following month, the Devlin Report on disturbances in Nyasaland, part of the Central African Federation, included a phrase (which captured the headlines) dubbing Nyasaland as, temporarily, 'a police state'.[7] Macmillan, after his impressive victory in the general election on 8 October 1959, appointed as colonial secretary the radical Tory Iain Macleod, who very soon scrapped the Colonial Office's gradualist timetable. At the end of his own tour through Ghana, Nigeria, Central Africa and South Africa, Macmillan addressed both Houses of the South African Parliament in Cape Town on 3 February 1960. Remembering that it was the Golden Jubilee of the formation of the Union, and stressing Britain's well-established investments and trade with South Africa, he went on to say that the most striking impression he had gained in his tour was the strength of African nationalism. 'The wind of change is blowing through this continent and, whether we like it or not, this growth of national consciousness is a political fact, ... and our national policies must take account of it.' He then moved on to more sensitive ground: 'We reject the idea of any inherent superiority of one race over another. Our policy is therefore non-racial.' While Britain would want to support South Africa, there were aspects of its policies which made it 'impossible for us to do this without being false to our own deep convictions about the political destinies of free men ...'[8] Later in the year, his former audience would vote for a republic and, in 1961, leave the Commonwealth.

While Macmillan was still in Africa, Iain Macleod was getting into his stride. He spent only two years at the Colonial Office, from October 1959 to October 1961, but they were the decisive years. Beginning somewhat flippantly with the remark that he hoped to be the 'last Colonial Secretary',[9] he went on to see five states become independent and gave the vital push towards majority rule to six more. By the summer of 1961, he was chairing five different constitutional conferences at the same time. The year 1960 saw the really significant break when Macleod showed himself willing to stand up to the white settler leaders in East and Central Africa. He was also vividly aware of rapid changes in the vast expanses westward in French and Belgian Africa.

After being elected President of the Fifth Republic in December 1958, General de Gaulle took tough military action briefly in Algeria and offered autonomy within the French community to France's tropical colonies. But when Guinea, which alone voted 'Non', went on to full independence and UN membership, de Gaulle found that the rest of French Africa would not be content with less. In an adroit *volte face* he granted independence to thirteen other colonies and planned negotiations for a settlement in Algeria, where bitter conflict had been under way since 1956. The other great turn-round was in the Congo, where the Belgians had concentrated on economic development and obstructed political advance. But on 1 July 1960 the Congo was granted independence and soon began to fall apart with a mutiny in the Belgian-officered Force Publique (which led to Belgian military intervention) and secession by Katanga (which led to UN police action).[10] To cap the year, on 14 December 1960 the United Nations General Assembly passed Resolution 1514 calling for a speedy end to colonialism. Thus, in a New Year survey for the Colonial Policy Committee, Macleod summarized his policies over 1960 as 'not as fast as the Congo and not as slow as Algiers',[11] though he still saw the risk of a Congo in Kenya and an Algeria in Central Africa. The real obstacles for Macleod were the white settler communities.

Macleod had visited East Africa in December 1959, and opened the Kenya constitutional conference in London in January 1960. While the Kenyan settlers had enjoyed the vote since 1919, the first African was not nominated to the legislative council until 1944. In 1948, when there were 30,000 Europeans, 120,000 Asians and 5 million Africans in Kenya, a new constitution incorporated a concept of 'balanced representation' – meaning the elected European members would equal the non-Europeans. At this time, the recently formed Kenya African Union was led by Jomo Kenyatta, the veteran Kikuyu leader who had lived in Britain for fifteen years. At the same time, some younger, more militant Kikuyu, soon labelled as 'Mau Mau', were exciting alarm by their activities.[12] In 1950, this movement was declared illegal; in 1952, a state of emergency was declared and African politics banned. Mau Mau then developed into an armed revolt by a 'Land Freedom Army' of up to 15,000 guerrillas, many of them veterans of the Burma campaign, and it took eleven British battalions to hold them down. In the process of suppressing the revolt, the authorities jailed Kenyatta along with thousands of Mau Mau detainees. The ministerial system, allowed in Kenya in 1954, was thus still dominated by Europeans, and there were no elections for African seats in the legislative council until 1957.

Macleod ended the Kenya emergency and pushed for African majority rule. At the constitutional conference in January 1960, he called for an African elected majority in the legislative council, and parity between Africans and non-Africans in the executive council. After elections in 1961, when two dominant African parties emerged, an African Leader of Government Business was appointed. In April 1961, Kenyatta was released and soon found a by-election seat. After a further election in 1963 (after Macleod had left the Colonial Office) Kenyatta became prime minister on 1 July, under full internal self-government. Independence for Kenya followed on 12 December 1963.

In Tanganyika independence came earlier and the path was smoother because there was only a small European population. Even so, no African was nominated to the legislative council until 1945, and under the member system, adopted in 1948, no Africans were given departmental charges. The idea of balancing Europeans and non-Europeans was also attempted here, but Tanganyika was a UN Trust Territory and in 1955 a visiting UN mission called for an African majority legislature. When the first elections were held in 1958–9, the Tanganyika African National Union, led by Julius Nyerere, won all the contested seats. Macleod was very impressed by Nyerere when he visited the Territory in 1959, and pushed for an African majority. Nyerere became chief minister after further elections in 1960, and at a constitutional conference held in Dar es Salaam in March 1961, Macleod announced the adoption of the style 'Prime Minister' under full internal self-government. Tanganyika became independent on 9 December 1961.[13]

Earlier in the same year, Macleod had also found an opportunity for disengaging from Uganda, the most puzzling of the East African territories. Uganda's development had been complicated by the role of the African kingdoms on the shores of Lake Victoria Nyanza, especially the privileged position of Buganda. In fact, Uganda's peculiar version of Indirect Rule had retarded political development. It was not until Sir Andrew Cohen (who had been influential in the Colonial Office in calling for the end of Indirect Rule) began to enlarge the legislative council in 1952 with a 'representative' element to balance the 'Government' side, that some political advance was made. Then in 1953 the pace quickened dramatically after the Kabaka of Buganda – fearful of an East African Federation on the Central African model – demanded independence for Buganda. Cohen decided to exile the youthful Kabaka to Britain, and in the aftermath of this crisis, the British Government sent the Australian Sir Keith Hancock to meet with an elected Ugandan Committee and with Cohen. An 'agreed memorandum' from these talks laid the basis for a new constitution, in 1955, which provided for a ministerial system with five unofficials in the executive council (three African, one European, and an Asian). But this was an interim arrangement; the make-up was to be adjustable with the sort of flexibility Cohen had mooted in 1947. Buganda would also be represented in the legislative council.

During the first elections in 1958, the largely Protestant Uganda People's Congress and largely Catholic Democratic Party did not show levels of support to indicate any basis yet for responsible government. Macleod now forced the pace. In 1961, elections were held under universal suffrage and the executive council was headed by a chief minister, Benedicto Kiwanuka of the Democratic Party. In 1962, full internal self-government was granted with Kiwanuka styled 'prime minister', though in new elections in April 1962 he was defeated by Milton Obote's Uganda People's Congress in alliance with a Buganda party. On 9 October 1962, Uganda gained independence with the Queen as head of state. One year later, the head of state became the President of Uganda, in the person of the Kabaka of Buganda. It seemed like a suitable fusion and reconciliation of traditional and modern, but it proved short-lived.[14]

Undoubtedly Macleod's most critical problem was the Central African Federation. The 60,000 Kenya settlers looked like a beleaguered minority beside the quarter-million whites ensconced in Central Africa, where in practice they held the reins of power. Southern Rhodesia had never been ruled directly from London. Settled originally by the British South Africa Company, its electors narrowly rejected the chance to join South Africa in 1922 and became, instead, a 'self-governing Colony' in a constitutional position not unlike the Dominions had had in the nineteenth century.[15] From 1926, the premier was invited as observer to the Imperial Conferences, and in 1933, given the title prime minister. Relations were handled by the Dominions Office (later the CRO). Before the 1939–45 war, there were numerous schemes for amalgamations and sub-divisions in Central Africa, which focused particularly on Southern Rhodesia's ambition to be linked to the Northern Rhodesian copper belt and the railway between the two. In Northern Rhodesia, which was a protectorate under the Colonial Office, the legislative council was dominated by the elected white unofficials, and in 1943 three of their number had been added to the executive council.

The Attlee Government resisted the demands of the Southern and Northern Rhodesian settler leaders for outright amalgamation, but in 1951 a scheme of federation was mooted which would retain territorial legislatures in the two Rhodesias and Nyasaland and include safeguards for Africans. At a critical stage in these proposals, Labour lost power, the

Conservatives came to office after the October 1951 general election, and two years later, as part of the 'New Elizabethan age' and Churchill's latter-day imperialism, the Federation of Rhodesia and Nyasaland went ahead, on 1 August 1953, against the opposition of the articulate Africans of the two protectorates and considerable public opposition in Britain. Decisions to federate were made in the three territorial legislative councils which were dominated by settlers. African nationalism in Central Africa focused on opposition to federation, demands for the franchise, and for African representation in the territorial legislatures.

This opposition quickened, in 1958, with the return of Dr Hastings Banda to Nyasaland, after an absence of forty-three years in South Africa, the USA, Britain and Ghana.[16] At the end of the year, Banda, along with Harry Nkumbula and Kenneth Kaunda (from Northern Rhodesia) and Joshua Nkomo (from Southern Rhodesia), attended an All-Africa Convention in Accra summoned by Nkrumah of Ghana, who called for an end to colonialism and planned, one day, to launch the United States of Africa. After Banda's return from Accra early in 1959, the Nyasaland Government and the federal authorities became convinced that murder and revolt were imminent in Nyasaland. In March 1959, Banda and Kaunda (in Northern Rhodesia), along with hundreds of their supporters, were detained. It was this Central African security crisis, along with the subsequent Hola camp killings in Kenya, and news of General de Gaulle's intended policy of independence for the expanses of French Africa, which convinced Macmillan that Britain must disengage, or risk further African emergencies and possible bloodshed which would suck in British troops, be politically damaging, and attract unwelcome attention in the United Nations. As well as appointing Macleod to the Colonial Office, Macmillan appointed a Royal Commission to review the federation.

Macleod insisted on the release of Banda, so he could give evidence to the Federal Review Commission. The colonial secretary was personally impressed by Banda and, at the Nyasaland constitutional conference in July–August 1960, conceded an African majority in the legislature. The first elections were held in August 1961, and a ministerial system was begun with Banda taking a ministerial post. At a further conference in November 1962, it was agreed that Nyasaland would receive full self-government with the right to leave the Federation. After elections in 1963, Banda became prime minister.

By now, federation seemed doomed, but the federal prime minister, Sir Roy Welensky, put up an obstinate and bitter fight to retain the linkage of the two Rhodesias and to cling to the resources of the copper belt and the entrenched position of the whites. Macleod had already realized that Northern Rhodesia was his most intractable problem, and when the federal review conference broke up in February 1961 without agreement, he had insisted on some immediate reform of the Northern Rhodesia constitution. As a first step, he sought parity between African and non-African seats in the legislature, and when Macmillan insisted on a compromise, giving less to Africans, violence followed in the copper belt. Kaunda warned that there might be a blood-bath which would make 'Mau Mau a child's picnic'.[17] He restrained his supporters with difficulty and in October 1962, an African coalition ministry was formed. At the constitutional conference in 1963 (after Macleod had gone), it was conceded that Northern Rhodesia could leave the Federation. Welensky, vilifying the Macmillan Government, tried final appeals, but on the last day of 1963 the Federation was dissolved. On 6 July 1964 Nyasaland became the Independent State of Malawi, while Northern Rhodesia became the Republic of Zambia on 24 October, leaving Southern Rhodesia (which had been a semi-Dominion since 1923) with a lesser status. This was all the more glaring in the light of recent changes in the criteria for Commonwealth membership following the independence of Cyprus and the break-up of the West Indies Federation.

Cyprus had acquired greater strategic significance after the decision in October 1954 to evacuate the Suez Canal Zone. But the earlier announcement that Cyprus was in the 'never' category for independence had excited the supporters of *Enosis* (union with Greece), who probably made up a majority of the 70 per cent Greek-speaking population. In 1955, the National Organization of Cypriot Fighters (EOKA) began a campaign of sabotage and terrorism, led by the conservative, puritanical Cypriot-born Greek, Colonel George Grivas. British reinforcements, the declaration of an emergency, the sending of Field Marshal Harding as Governor, and the exile of Archbishop Makarios, the Greek Cypriot leader, all failed to extinguish EOKA. After the Suez fiasco, Macmillan decided Britain should contemplate partition or independence in return for retention of its bases. Makarios was released (much to the disgust of Tory die-hard Lord Salisbury) and the Archbishop gave up the goal of *Enosis* in favour of independence (much to the disgust of Grivas). By an agreement, signed on 19 February 1959, between Makarios and the British, Turkish, and Greek Governments, Cyprus was set to become a sovereign independent republic in 1960, with Britain retaining two small Sovereign Base Areas at Akrotiri and

Dhekelia. This settlement, backed by three Nato members, removed a festering sore on the Western flank in the Cold War, but it posed an immediate problem for the Commonwealth.

Could such a small country, with a population of only 500,000, become a fully equal Commonwealth member? The Cyprus agreement, in fact, reopened yet again the question of the future of the smaller colonies. Macmillan still hoped that a mezzanine status could be devised. External association on the Eire model was reconsidered and the concept of 'Commonwealth Statehood' similar to Singapore's was revisited. But early in 1960, while Macmillan was on his 'Wind of Change' tour, Makarios and his Turkish Cypriot colleagues made it clear that Cyprus would not be part of any '2nd Eleven'. So the matter was put to the 1960 Commonwealth Prime Ministers' Meetings, where the New Zealand prime minister threw more fat in the fire by announcing that he was negotiating for the independence of the Trust Territory of Western Samoa with a population of 100,000. Menzies, Nehru and others realized that Cyprus would create a precedent, and the matter was therefore sent to a Commonwealth study group of senior officials. In preparation for their deliberations Macmillan had an intimate talk with Macleod, Lord Home (the Commonwealth Secretary) and Sir Norman Brook, on 13 July 1960, where it was accepted that if Cyprus were admitted as a full member of the Commonwealth 'then all the other tiddlers would demand this treatment'.[18] When the study group met at Chequers in July 1960 the British delegate expressed a worry that Western Samoa might create an even worse precedent, but his New Zealand colleague indicated that Samoa would probably not seek to join either the Commonwealth or the United Nations.

The study group concluded that it would be 'a frustration of much that the Commonwealth stands for' if a small country, on attaining independence, were denied membership.[19] Full independence, with equal membership, was the outcome most consistent with the aspirations of new nations and the ethos of the Commonwealth. Therefore, Cyprus became an independent republic on 10 August 1960 and, with the approval of the heads of government, was represented at the Prime Ministers' Meetings in March 1961. New Year's Day 1962 was set for the inauguration of the Independent State of Western Samoa. From the CRO came the fear that if it became a candidate for Commonwealth membership 'This ... would be a reductio ad absurdum, and we are counting on New Zealand to nurse the Samoans along in such a way as to stave off any application of this kind.'[20] To their relief, the first independent Pacific Island state did not apply for membership at this stage, and Macmillan sent a goodwill message for the independence celebrations.

Cyprus provided the landmark precedent and was followed in 1962 by Jamaica (population 1.5 million) and Trinidad (population 0.75 million). This spelt the end of the West Indies Federation for which independence had been expected about the same time. Macleod regarded the West Indies as his greatest failure. The ten-member Federation had come into being in February 1958. Plans for an independence bill were advanced in 1960 and Macleod went to the Caribbean to meet island leaders. Here, he was made aware of the growing dissatisfaction in Jamaica, the largest member, over the distribution of federal financial burdens, which led the chief minister to announce a referendum over Jamaica's membership. This prospect overshadowed the constitutional conference held in May 1961, when Eric Williams, the Trinidad chief minister, indicated that his country might also reconsider its membership. When the Jamaicans voted in September 1961, 54 per cent to 46 per cent in favour of quitting the Federation, Macleod agreed that, in view of the Cyprus precedent, Jamaica should go on to independence, which was granted on 2 August 1962. Williams said that '1 from 10 leaves 0' and Trinidad followed, on 31 August 1962, the same day the Federation was formally dissolved.[21] Hopes for a federation of the eastern 'Little Eight' islands came to nothing.

Failure in the Caribbean was balanced by a seeming success in Southeast Asia, where there had long been proposals for unifying Malaya, Singapore and the Borneo territories. The separation of Malaya and Singapore, since 1946, had broken up the complementary economy of the rich commodity-producing peninsula and entrepôt port. Independence for the Federation of Malaya in 1957, and statehood for Singapore in 1959, accentuated this separation and soon opened up Cold War perils. For, at the very moment the emergency in Malaya ended, on 31 July 1960, the politics of Singapore swung to the left and there were fears of a Southeast Asian Cuba. Thus, in a speech in Singapore on 27 May 1961, Tengku Abdul Rahman, the Malayan prime minister, advocated a 'merger' between Singapore and Malaya. Moreover, as Singapore's predominantly Chinese population would create a slight Chinese majority in a merger, he added the British North Borneo territories – the Crown colonies of Sarawak and North Borneo and the protected state of Brunei – as part of the proposed new 'Malaysia'.

Agreement in principle was reached between Singapore and Malaya in November 1961, and the British welcomed the opportunity to unload their recently acquired Borneo territories provided that local opinion approved. In 1962, a joint commission, under Lord Cobbold, found reasonable support for the proposal: this was later confirmed by a UN mission. A referendum was held in Singapore in September 1962. Favourable votes were cast in the legislatures of Sarawak and North Borneo. However, a short-lived revolt in Brunei in December 1962 so shook the Sultan that he stood aloof from Malaysia and clung to his protectorate status. By the Malaysia Agreement of 9 July 1963, Britain relinquished sovereignty over Singapore, Sarawak, and North Borneo, which became states in the Federation of Malaysia. It also agreed to continue support in external defence and to station forces in association with Australia and New Zealand in the new Malaysia, which commenced its existence on 16 September 1963.[22]

Three other small territories also found a future in association with neighbours and therefore avoided any immediate question of Commonwealth membership. In the Horn of Africa, British Somaliland became independent and united with former Italian Somaliland to form the Republic of Somalia in 1960. This represented the quickest policy transition of the breathless 'African year'. The Somali peoples were largely pastoralists who spread over a large area of northern Kenya, the Ogaden and Haud regions of Ethiopia, and French, British, and Italian Somaliland. At the end of the 1939–45 war, all but the French enclave were under British military occupation, including parts of Ethiopia whose government had been restored in 1942. As part of his policy for disposing of the former Italian colonies, Ernest Bevin had, in 1946, pressed for unification of all the Somali lands. The Somalis, for their part, having learnt about the *Risorgimento* in their Italian colonial schools, readily responded to the idea of unification. However, Ethiopia would not agree and the UN General Assembly voted, in 1949, to confer on Italy a ten-year trusteeship over its former colony to expire in 1960. In 1954, the British handed over the Haud hinterland to Ethiopia in return for guarantees of Somali grazing rights.

Politics in British Somaliland developed around demands for the return of the Haud lands and for political advances in step with those in the Italian Trust Territory. Yet the British were hanging on to their problematical protectorate for strategic Cold War reasons. As the Italians imported Arabic-speaking teachers from Egypt for their schools, there were fears, in the post-Suez atmosphere, that Egyptian influence would be a herald of Russian influence, which would threaten Kenya. If the Sudan came under similar influences there would be the possibility of 'a pincer movement threatening all our East African territories'.[23] The Colonial Office was slow to implement change, but announced in 1956 that a legislative council would be created in 1957, and independence might be considered after 1960. Yet, as the Italians moved towards the end of their trusteeship, Britain had to advance the pace in its protectorate. In 1959, elections were held for the legislative council and, in 1960, a ministerial system began. Only few months later, on 26 June, independence was granted, which was followed on 1 July by independence for Italian Somaliland when the two were united in the Somali Republic.

Somewhat similar moves followed in the West African Trust Territory of the British Cameroons where plebiscites were held in February 1961. As small portions of the former German colony of Kamerun, the non-contiguous territories of Northern Cameroons and Southern Cameroons had been Mandates, later UN Trust Territories, administered as part of Nigeria. But when Nigeria became independent in 1960, they remained detached. In the 1961 plebiscites, Northern Cameroons chose to join Nigeria. Southern Cameroons, which had its own legislature and feared Igbo expansionism from Eastern Nigeria, opted to join the former French Trust Territory, now the Cameroon Republic. The union took place on 1 October 1961.[24]

Decolonization in East Africa also included the island of Zanzibar, which had a largely African population but was ruled by an Arab dynasty under British protection and advice. Macleod sent a constitutional commission in 1960; an elected majority was granted in the legislative council and a chief minister appointed. Universal suffrage was adopted in 1962 and full internal self-government followed in June 1963. This sudden, largely unsought, advance prompted the minority Arab ruling groups in Zanzibar to organize and accept the end of British protection before the Afro-Shirazi Party could mobilize the African majority. Thus, in the 1963 elections an Arab-led coalition won a majority of seats in the legislature, without gaining a majority of the popular vote. The British transferred power on 10 December 1963 and the Sultan became head of state in independent Zanzibar. A month later he was toppled by an African-organized coup on the night of 11/12 January 1964 and a revolutionary council took over. In April 1964, the new regime made an agreement with Nyerere of Tanganyika and the Union of Tanzania was created.

Zanzibar was the sixteenth dependency to become independent since Macmillan had taken over the government in the aftermath of Suez. It was soon followed by Zambia and Malawi and also by Malta, which, along with Gibraltar and Cyprus, made up the trio of rare European colonies. Although it had long enjoyed representative institutions, Malta had, on several occasions, reverted to direct rule. Self-government, restored in 1947, with a prime minister and Cabinet, was not followed by Dominion status when requested in the 1950s, although integration with Britain was seriously entertained. However, in the aftermath of this abortive scheme, political disorders in the island heralded another return to Governor's rule and, by the time representative government was restored in 1962, the Macleod acceleration was well under way. Britain continued to control external affairs and defence because of Malta's importance as a Nato base, but the Maltese began to demand independence. A constitutional conference in 1963 failed to get agreement but after a new conference session in 1964 and a referendum, Malta became independent on 21 September 1964.

At Macmillan's first Prime Ministers' Meetings in 1957, there had been nine members – Australia, Britain, Canada, Ceylon, Ghana, India, New Zealand, Pakistan and South Africa – plus Central Africa as an observer. By the time the Conservatives relinquished power to Harold Wilson's Labour Government on 16 October 1964, the number had more than doubled, South Africa had left, and Southern Rhodesia was not invited.

5

WILSON AND THE WITHDRAWAL FROM EAST-OF-SUEZ, 1966–76

Labour returned to power in Britain in October 1964 after thirteen years in opposition. Harold Wilson's distinctive contributions to decolonization were the 'Withdrawal from East-of-Suez' and failure to prevent Southern Rhodesia's UDI. Yet, just as Macmillan had started his premiership determined not to preside over the liquidation of the Empire, and waited two years before bowing to the 'Wind of Change', so Wilson began by proclaiming Britain's frontiers as the Himalayas and by reaffirming the East-of-Suez role. Indeed, Labour's approach in the early 1960s had echoes of the expansive mood of Ernest Bevin. Macmillan's first application to join the EEC had been attacked in 1962 by Hugh Gaitskell, then leader of the party, with the cry: 'It means the end of a thousand years of history. You may say, "Let it end", but, my goodness, it is a decision that needs a little care and thought. And it does mean the end of the Commonwealth.'[1]

At Wilson's first party conference after becoming leader in 1963, he talked of establishing 'new industries which would make us once again one of the foremost industrial nations of the world'. It was to be done by 're-stating our Socialism in terms of the scientific revolution'. A revived Britain would be 'forged in the white heat of this revolution' so that outdated methods would be banished, distinctions between 'Gentlemen and Players' ended, and latent talents released 'to ensure Britain's standing in the world'.[2] When he came to power in 1964, with a slender majority of five in the Commons, Wilson reaffirmed support for the United States in the Cold War by offering diplomatic (but not military) support for American intervention in Vietnam and, as part of this continuing alignment, he said we 'cannot afford to relinquish our East of

Suez role'. The Malayan Emergency had been successfully concluded in 1960, Kuwait saved from an Iraqi threat in 1963, post-independence mutinies in East African armies curbed in 1964, and Indonesia's Confrontation of the new Malaysia was being held off. Introducing the Defence White Paper of 1965, defence secretary Denis Healey said it would be 'politically irresponsible and economically wasteful' to abandon Aden, which had recently become the Middle East military headquarters.[3] Thus, in general strategy, there was considerable continuity with the post-Suez posture of maintaining a limited world-power role.

Decolonization, though not deliberately accelerated by Labour at this time, nevertheless had achieved steadily growing momentum from the Macleod years. It was moving inexorably along the now well-signalled route through adjustments to executive and legislative councils, elections held under universal suffrage, dyarchy and member system, followed by ministerial system, leading to responsible government (now called full internal self-government) with constitutional conferences in London, pre-independence elections and, finally, transfer of power to elected, if sometimes tenuous, regimes who had their joyous flag ceremonies and independence day celebrations. The process which had for the Dominions taken eighty years, India thirty years, Ghana ten years, and Malaya two years, had, by the 1960s, become tightly telescoped. The leap from first democratic election to independence was usually only circumscribed by the effort of getting local agreement about electoral arrangements, the need to draft the appropriate constitutional instruments, and to erect rudimentary structures of Cabinet rule.

During Labour's first two years, nine more countries gained independence according to timetables already published. The last and smallest of the West African territories, The Gambia (population 0.5 million) had had an unofficial element in the executive council following Gold Coast/Nigerian models since the 1940s. A ministerial system was adopted after general elections in 1960; a chief minister was appointed, who was titled premier in 1962, and prime minister in 1963, under full internal self-government. Independence followed on 18 October 1965. The problem colony of the Caribbean, British Guiana, had had self-government restored in 1957, when Dr Jagan, the leader dismissed in 1953, became a minister. In 1961, under a new constitution, he finally became premier. The principle of independence was conceded, in 1962, but the chief party, the People's Progressive Party, split into predominantly Afro-American and East-Indian wings, and the constitutional conference was bedevilled by ethnic and ideological differences, which also erupted into disorder in the colony necessitating the continued presence of British troops. In the end, it was left to the Colonial Office to devise an electoral system, which was done by the expedient of announcing, in October 1963, a system of proportional representation. Elections in December 1964 produced a coalition of the Afro wing of the PPP, now the People's National Congress, and the United Force. The final constitutional conference in November 1965, even though boycotted by Jagan, agreed on independence for Guyana on 26 May 1966.[4]

In Southern Africa, Britain also disengaged from the three High Commission Territories, which had once been coveted by South Africa. Indeed, in the 1956 report recommending extending apartheid by the erection of 'Bantustans', Basutoland, Bechuanaland and Swaziland had been included as part of the project. But in 1960 South Africa shocked the world with the Sharpeville massacre, left the Commonwealth in the following year, and became increasingly isolated. Britain moved quickly to perform its decolonization drills in the three territories. In 1965, Bechuanaland's capital was shifted from Mafeking (in Cape Province) to Gaborone and, in 1963, the protectorate was detached from the High Commissioner's control and placed under its own Commissioner. Elections under universal suffrage were held in 1964, and self-government, with a prime minister and responsible Cabinet, began in 1965. On 30 September 1966, the Republic of Botswana became independent. Basutoland followed quickly on its heels. A constitutional commission, appointed in 1962, produced proposals which were accepted by the Basutoland National Council and by a constitutional conference in 1964. The first elections followed in 1965 and independence was achieved by the Kingdom of Lesotho on 4 October 1966. In the other southern kingdom, Swaziland, the performance was slightly varied. High Commission control was ended in 1963 and executive and legislative councils were created in the next year. In 1967, Swaziland became a Protected State, with paramount Chief Sobhuza II (who had reigned since 1921) recognized as king and head of state. Independence followed on 6 September 1968. In all these cases, decolonization was negotiated by transfers of power – albeit extremely hasty transfers by the standards of twenty (even ten) years earlier.

In Rhodesia, UDI on 11 November 1965 meant the one serious breach in the sequence of negotiated decolonization. Southern Rhodesia had, of course, never been ruled directly from London. As a chartered company territory, self-governing colony from 1923, and member of the Central African Federation 1953–63, Southern Rhodesia was always an anomaly and its white settler minority (numbering about 200,000) was accustomed to self-government and even observer status at Imperial and Commonwealth councils. In 1964, on the eve of Labour's victory, Malawi and Zambia had become independent and Rhodesia was not invited by Sir Alec Douglas-Home (Macmillan's successor) to take the former federal observer's seat at the PMMs of that year. Rebuffed in its requests for a negotiated recognition of independence, the Rhodesian Front Government of Ian Smith detained many African national leaders and threatened unilateral action. Labour ministers, and Wilson himself, visited Salisbury in attempts to dissuade the Rhodesians. Five fairly generous principles were put forward as criteria for independence: a franchise leading to eventual majority rule; guarantees that the constitution would not be abrogated; an immediate increase of African political rights; an end to discriminatory legislation; and assurances that the Constitution was acceptable to the majority. It was argued at the time that Wilson's stand was a weak one, in that the five principles did not require immediate majority rule as an essential condition. The possibility of Britain using force against an illegal declaration of independence was also ruled out. Some believed that the Rhodesian security forces would not have resisted the Queen's forces, but Wilson (with his slender parliamentary majority) was, in turn, apprehensive about 'kith and kin Tories' and possible objections within the British forces, and therefore left Ian Smith free to act. Rhodesia became a running sore for the Labour Government and a disruptive issue for the Commonwealth. Negotiations to seek a compromise, held on HMS *Tiger* in 1966, failed, even though Wilson was still prepared to recognize independence *before* majority rule. By the second attempt, on HMS *Fearless* in 1968, Wilson had raised his terms to 'No Independence Before Majority African Rule', NIBMAR,[5] and failure was almost a foregone conclusion. Sanctions, which Wilson once said rashly would succeed in 'weeks rather than months', failed to curb the Rhodesians, who evaded a naval blockade with South African help. In the end, a fifteen-year guerrilla war and a coup in Portugal were necessary to dislodge the white regime.

If UDI delayed decolonization in the notorious case of Rhodesia, devaluation accelerated it East-of-Suez. Here the future of Britain's military bases in Aden and Singapore, of the island colonies in the Indian Ocean, and of the oil-rich Protected States in the Arabian/Persian Gulf and Brunei, had yet to be determined.

A potentially complicating factor was the failure of the Malaysia –

Singapore merger. Although the creation of Malaysia in 1963 had seemed an appropriate solution to Britain's untidy legacy in Southeast Asia, ideological differences between the ruling Alliance Party in Malaya and the People's Action Party (PAP) in Singapore became insuperable. Lee Kuan Yew, the dynamic young Singapore leader, took the merger seriously to the extent of calling for a 'Malaysian Malaysia' and the PAP ran candidates on the peninsula in the 1964 general elections. Although it only managed to win one seat, the campaign gave rise to serious race riots and fears that Singapore would be expelled from the Federation. Thus Singapore agreed to withdraw and, on 7 August 1965, the respective prime ministers signed a separation agreement, recognizing Singapore's sovereignty. Two days later, Singapore (which had been denied Dominion status in the pre-Cyprus days, ten years before) became an independent republic.[6] Since it was estimated that about 20 per cent of the island's economy depended on the British military presence, Britain's future defence policy had severe implications for the new mini-state.

In February 1966, Denis Healey announced the results of the Labour Government's major defence review. This was revised in July 1967, and the proposed changes were accelerated in January 1968. In this way, the policy of maintaining Britain's position East-of-Suez was progressively reversed and became instead one of 'Withdrawal from East-of-Suez'. The review began as an exercise in matching resources and commitments. In 1966, British defence expenditure was running at 7 per cent of GNP, and Healey's aim was to reduce it to 6 per cent by the end of the decade. To this end, new aircraft projects and new aircraft carriers were cancelled, the Aden base was to be closed, Middle East headquarters were moved yet again, to Bahrain, and British forces in Malaysia and Singapore would be reduced. But Britain would retain a military 'presence' in Southeast Asia (in association with Australia and New Zealand) and would retain a Singapore base as long as required. In July 1967, however, a timetable was inserted into the rundown. Britain would now retain not a 'presence', but a 'military capability', after the mid-1970s. To facilitate this, a staging-base strategy was under consideration partly as an economy measure, but also partly as a response to events in the Middle East (where overflying rights were in doubt) and partly in connection with decolonization in the Indian Ocean colonies.

In November 1965, a new dependency was created entitled British Indian Ocean Territory (BIOT) consisting of the Chagos Archipelago (midway between Zanzibar and Singapore) and three islands lying north of Madagascar, which were part of the Seychelles. Staging-bases on these islands would supplement the airstrip constructed on Gan in the Maldives in 1960, since this might become untenable following independence granted to the Maldives on 26 July 1965. Thus the Chagos Archipelago was detached from Mauritius in the run-up to its independence. It was agreed at the Mauritius constitutional conference in September 1965 that Britain would pay Mauritius £3 million and the new state would recolonize about a thousand islanders from Diego Garcia. Mauritius advanced to internal self-government in 1967 and became independent on 12 March 1968. The islands of Aldabra, Des Roches, and Farquahar, which were under consideration for a staging-base, were three of the more than 100 islands which made up the colony of the Seychelles and were now detached and incorporated in the BIOT in 1965. Aldabra appeared as the likely site for a 12,000-foot runway and fuel store, but this 'Abracadabra strategy' soon encountered the opposition of environmentalists in Britain and the United States who campaigned to protect the Indian Ocean's main breeding ground for frigate birds. In January 1968 (in the wake of the devaluation crisis of November 1967), Abracadabra evaporated and withdrawal from Singapore and Malaysia was postponed until mid-1971.[7] On 8 December 1968, the management of the Singapore naval base was handed over to the Singapore Government.

As it turned out, the departure from Singapore was delayed because of the return to power of the Conservatives under Edward Heath in 1970. Instead of completing the departure from the base, the Conservative Government negotiated a Five Power Defence Arrangement (FPDA) with Malaysia, Singapore, Australia and New Zealand, in 1971, whereby an ANZUK fleet would be stationed in Singapore and an integrated air defence system for Malaysia be created. However, when Labour returned to power in 1974, the withdrawal recommenced, although the FPDA was not rescinded. By 1976, the British had withdrawn their troops from Southeast Asia except for small garrisons in Hong Kong and Brunei. In the latter case, the bills were paid by the oil-rich Sultanate, which by an agreement of November 1971 ceased to be a Protected State. Britain continued for a further decade to assist Brunei with external affairs and defence, but an agreement was made in 1979 to phase out these responsibilities, and the Sultanate of Brunei Darussalam became a fully independent state on 31 December 1983. The relics of the Indian Ocean 'Abracadabra strategy' were also dismantled. Diego Garcia became the site of a British–American communications facility and later US storage, refuelling and maintenance units. Aldabra and the other unused parts of the BIOT reverted to Seychelles when it became independent on 29 June 1976.

In Aden and the Gulf States, Britain's departure was more precipitate. Aden, as the finest natural harbour between Suez and Ceylon, was a major maritime bunkering place, site of a large oil refinery and, from 1961, the headquarters of British Middle East forces. Aden Colony was a cosmopolitan port city, quite different and separate from its Arabian hinterland made up of the Eastern and Western Aden Protectorates, where a version of Indirect Rule had operated under the authority of advisory treaties signed with the local sheikhs. In the 1950s, Aden was one of those territories in the 'never' category for independence. Yet, after the Suez fiasco of 1956, there was increasing anti-British propaganda emanating from Cairo, and a South Arabian League in Aden called for the combination of colony and protectorate and eventual unification with the Arab state of Yemen. In 1960, an imaginative Governor suggested adopting the Singapore or Cyprus model – that Britain should relinquish sovereignty over Aden and secure use of the base by treaty. But British policy was directed firstly at federating the protectorate tribes and then, in 1963, the colony and the hinterland were combined in the Federation of South Arabia. In 1964, a constitutional conference was held and there was talk of independence by 1968. These plans were overtaken by the devaluation crisis and by civil war between rival groups in Aden. In November 1967, the British suddenly withdrew from Aden, leaving their stores behind.[8] A People's Republic of South Yemen was established in the wake of a scuttle even more precipitate than the abandonment of the Palestine Mandate twenty years before.

At the time of the Aden evacuation, the Government said it would not abandon the Protected States of the Gulf, but it changed its mind two months later. Along with the announcement of withdrawal from Singapore by 1971 came a similar warning in respect of the Gulf States. Another rapid about-turn had been induced by the pressure of events.

The term 'British Protected States' had been adopted, in 1949, for the ten sheikhdoms which have been described by Glen Balfour-Paul as 'unique curiosities, even by imperial Britain's standards of curiosity'. They were (from north to south) Kuwait, Bahrain, Qatar, Abu Dhabi, Dubai, Sharjah, Ajmar, Umm al-Qaiwain, Ras al-Khaimah and Fujairah, and were a legacy of the Bombay Marine's imposition of a 'maritime truce' on the Gulf coasts in the mid-nineteenth century. Responsibility had been transferred from India to the Foreign Office after the 1939–45 war, when the British Residency was transferred from the Iran coast to Bahrain. A British-led force, the Trucial Oman Levies, also existed at brigade strength. In the 1950s, it was expected that any suggestion of independence in the Gulf would be at least twenty years away.

Protected State status was first ended in Kuwait, whose independent sovereignty was recognized by Britain on 19 June 1961, and when it was threatened by Iraq in the following year, British forces returned briefly to deter the Iraqis. Protection was soon taken over by Arab League forces. In 1965, Britain proposed that the remaining nine states should federate, but little progress was achieved in this direction. The sudden announcement of withdrawal in 1968 shook the Gulf sheikhs. Two opted for independence on the Kuwait model, Bahrain and Qatar becoming sovereign states on 17 August and 3 September 1971 respectively. Five of the remaining small states on the Trucial Coast came together as the United Arab Emirates and two more joined in 1972,[9] thus completing Britain's final withdrawal from the Arab world, that last and most troublesome region of Empire and the one un-represented in the Commonwealth. By this time, the Commonwealth itself was undergoing significant change, including experimentation with an alternative to full membership for small self-governing colonies.

The major change was the creation of the Commonwealth Secretariat in 1965 and the Commonwealth Foundation a year later. Thereafter the machinery of consultation, co-operation, and information-sharing shifted around the corner from Whitehall to Pall Mall where it was taken on by the Secretariat established in Marlborough House. The Founda-tion was designed to foster professional links at the non-governmental level. The Commonwealth was now centred on institutions shared by the member countries collectively. The first Secretary-General, Arnold Smith, a Canadian, set about establishing the Commonwealth's image as something different from the Empire.[10] At the same time, the long-standing endeavour to cater for very small dependencies produced the concepts of 'associated statehood' and 'special membership' in a new context.

The pioneering, in this development, was done by New Zealand in relation to the Cook Islands, which had a population of about 20,000, many of whom lived in New Zealand. In 1962, four options were offered to the Cook Islanders: independence, integration into New Zealand, a Pacific Islands federation, or self-government in 'free association' with New Zealand. The Cook Islands chose the last option by a referendum in 1964, which was observed by a UN mission. Under the new constitution, the Queen (as Queen of New Zealand) remained head of state, while a premier and Cabinet became responsible to the assembly. External relations and defence would be conducted in consultation with the New Zealand prime minister.[11] This model of voluntary 'associated status' was also tried by the British for the small Caribbean islands in the wake of the failure of the West Indies Federation.

It had been hoped that an East Caribbean Federation of the 'Little Eight' might be possible, but in 1965 Antigua withdrew from the negotiations and in 1966 Barbados opted for independence. The latter had long enjoyed a measure of self-government and possessed one of the oldest representative legislatures outside Europe, dating from 1639. Since the 1880s, the executive council had met with assemblymen in an executive committee to provide a link between executive and legislature. A member system, dyarchy, universal suffrage and ministerial system had been steadily granted, culminating in full internal self-government by 1961. Barbados had also supplied the federal prime minister. In a constitutional conference in April 1965, it was agreed that full independence would follow on 30 November 1966.

In the smaller Antilles, the Cook Islands model was tried by way of the West Indies Act of 1967 which provided that each island would have an executive responsible to an elected-majority legislature; there would be a shared Supreme Court, and a single British representative based on St Lucia. British law could not apply in the islands unless 'requested and consented to'. With the islands enjoying self-government in internal affairs, Britain would remain responsible for defence and external affairs. This new status of 'free and voluntary association' would be terminable by a two-thirds majority in the legislature or a referendum. The Caribbean Associated States were Antigua, Grenada, Dominica, St Kitts–Nevis–Anguilla, St Lucia, and St Vincent. But the arrangement was short-lived; from the mid-1970s the islands opted, slowly, one by one, for full independence. In one notorious case, Anguilla, there was a more unusual outcome. The 6,000 Anguillans resented subordination to St Kitts and in 1967 expelled their Kittian policemen and talked of independence. Various missions from neighbouring states and Britain were rejected and in 1969 a republic was proclaimed. At this point, the Wilson Government, which had balked at using force in Rhodesia, had no compunction in dispatching two frigates and landing 300 paratroops and forty London bobbies, whose most serious injuries were from sunburn. Rule by a Commissioner for Anguilla as a separate dependency followed.

As if to underline the growing realization that small islands could make big headlines, the case of Nauru, in the Central Pacific, provided yet another model of Commonwealth decolonization. Nauru had been a phosphate-rich German colony, captured by Australians in the 1914–18 war and administered by them as agents of a combined Mandate conferred by the League of Nations in 1920 on Australia, Britain and New Zealand jointly. The British Phosphate Commission, which worked the phosphate, sold it to Australian and New Zealand farmers at a fraction of the world price. In so doing, it was depleting the Nauruans' great asset. Eventually the islanders faced the prospect of a devastated landscape and declining resources. After the island became a UN Trust Territory following the 1939–45 war, Nauru chiefs appealed to the UN in the 1950s for a greater say in their government. They then asserted ownership of the phosphate in their land and demanded their independence on the island or elsewhere. Possible resettlement sites were considered in the Solomon Islands, Fiji, New Guinea or off the Queensland Coast, but by 1964 all had been rejected. Although independence for a population of 6,000 was regarded as ridiculous, Australia found that Nauru and its Trust Territory in New Guinea were becoming an embarrassment in the UN. The three trustee countries agreed to vest the phosphate operations in a locally owned Nauru Phosphate Corporation and on 31 January 1968, the Republic of Nauru became the first of the micro-states.[12] But it did not join the Commonwealth, becoming instead the first 'Special Member' which could participate in some Commonwealth programmes but not the political meetings.

6

CLOSING THE FILES ON THE PACIFIC, CARIBBEAN AND SOUTHERN AFRICA

The year 1971 provided the penultimate watershed in Britain's decolonization. In January came the Singapore conference – the first new-style summit meeting, now titled 'Commonwealth Heads of Government Meeting' (CHOGM), and held outside London. Not only was the first CHOGM notable for its title, venue and chairmanship by the Singaporean prime minister Lee Kuan Yew, but it broke new ground in three other respects.

First, it presaged a new coherence in the association by the adoption of the Commonwealth Declaration of Principles and by the approval of the creation of the Commonwealth Fund for Technical Co-operation.[1] Secondly, the Pacific Island states of Western Samoa, Tonga, and Fiji attended for the first time. Thirdly, the Queen was advised by Edward Heath, the British prime minister, to stay away because Britain would be in bad odour for failing to end Rhodesia's UDI and for selling arms to South Africa. This distancing of Britain from the rest of the Commonwealth was symbolized vividly later in 1971 when, on 28 October, the House of Commons voted in favour of Britain's entry into the European Economic Community (EEC). On that very day the Royal Assent was added to a new Commonwealth Immigration Bill designed to tighten restrictions on non-white migration into Britain. If the 1960s had been the decade of agonizing about disengagement-before-bloodshed, about the criteria for membership of the Commonwealth, and about whether or not to 'enter Europe', the 1970s would be the years when most of the remnants of Empire were discharged and the files closed on the Pacific, the Caribbean, and Southern Africa.

The Pacific territories were the last to be considered as ripe for decolonization. In all the earlier discussions about the future of smaller territories, the Pacific Islands were at the bottom of the list, always in the 'never' category. For the 1951 concept of 'City or Island States', only Fiji was seen as qualifying. In Macmillan's profit and loss study of 1957, no demands for constitutional change were reported from Fiji and Tonga. The British Solomon Islands Protectorate and the Gilbert and Ellice Islands Colony were marked at the earliest stages of political evolution. For the 1959 proposal of 'Commonwealth Statehood', it was thought that Fiji might be ready in ten years' time. After Sir Andrew Cohen heard in Wellington before the 1960 PMM of New Zealand's plans for Western Samoa, there was a flurry of anxiety and a CRO official said that Britain was 'particularly interested in avoiding a precedent which would lead to demands for unqualified independence by our own smaller colonial territories, and to the further dilution of the United Nations by States too small to support independent statehood'.[2] Yet, for all this caution, the Pacific could not be isolated from general trends.

Macmillan himself had turned to the Pacific because of prompting from an unusual quarter. In 1959, the Duke of Edinburgh passed on some impressions he had gained during a visit to the Pacific and to Hong Kong, which led Macmillan to call a ministerial meeting at No. 10 and to set senior officials to study the problem.[3] At this point, the Foreign Office and Treasury suggested Britain should 'divest' itself of these responsibilities; the CRO wanted to call in help from Australia and New Zealand, but the Colonial Office resisted the call to get rid of the territories. Sir Hilton Poynton, one of the Deputy Under-secretaries, expressed his discomfiture on the eve of the Macleod whirlwind:

> The task of 'Empire-unbuilding' is a difficult one. I don't mind 'giving up' a territory when it becomes independent – Ghana, Malaya, Nigeria etc. I don't mind 'giving up' a territory in favour of another Commonwealth administration if that provides a more efficient administration and is what the people want. I *do* object to being asked to 'give up' territories just because they are thought to be a nuisance to the Treasury and others![4]

The Cabinet, however, appointed an inter-departmental committee on Pacific future policy, which worked between 1961 and 1963 to gather information about the plans of the other colonial powers in the Pacific and consider future options. There were also annual consultations in Singapore between British representatives in the Far East and Pacific, Anglo-Australian discussions at Canberra, and a study group from

Australia, New Zealand and the United States held in Washington in 1963.

The chief cause of concern in the early 1960s, as decolonization gathered speed in Africa, was that the Pacific could be cast as the 'last stronghold of colonialism'.[5] Soviet representatives at the UN began to take an interest in places like Papua New Guinea, and to cultivate representatives from the islands. Lord Selkirk, the Commissioner-General in Southeast Asia, visited Fiji and New Zealand in 1961, and reported with some alarm that 'the Cold War front is advancing upon Oceania'.[6] Yet full independence was still ruled out. The islands were all thought to need some sort of attachment to a larger country. The aim was to 'keep the Communists out of the Pacific'. There was airy talk of Melanesian federation, a 'Hawaiian solution' (integration), or a 'Western Samoan solution' (independence without membership of international forums).[7] In 1963, the Washington study group suggested the only likely candidates for independence were Fiji, Tonga and Papua New Guinea.

Fiji, with a population of half a million, was Britain's major headache, but when Nigel Fisher, minister of state in the Colonial Office, visited Fiji in 1963, he reported that close links with Britain were still desired. Fiji's great problem was that, although by the 1874 cession, Fijians had retained the ownership of all land and lived under a pioneer system of Indirect Rule through village, district, and provincial chiefs under a Fijian administration (including consultation of the Great Council of Chiefs by the Governor), the majority population, since 1946, were Indians, descendants of indentured labourers brought in between 1879 and 1916. The constitution, dating from 1937, allowed domination by the small, three-thousand-strong, white settler population who were chiefly Australians. Although official majorities were maintained in the ruling councils, the legislative council included six European and three Indian elected members and three Fijians nominated by the Great Council of Chiefs. Of these, one European, one Indian and one Fijian were appointed to the executive council.[8] But any political advance involved a decision about the ratio of Fijians to Indians and it was feared premature withdrawal might lead to civil war, communist intervention, and Fiji becoming a 'potential Cuba'.[9]

Lord Selkirk's first inclination in 1961 was to present alternatives not unlike Wavell's for India in 1946. They could 'get out of Fiji' and let the people fight it out and, to be fairer to the Fijians, this should be sooner rather than later, so that they would not be hopelessly outnumbered. Another possibility was to involve New Zealand in the administration, or Britain could make it clear that it would stay indefinitely and lay down clear conditions.[10] But, after the Singapore discussions of 1962, Selkirk suggested simply informing the Indians that Fijians would retain entrenched rights, according to long-standing commitments, and that, if the Indians did not like it, 'they had better go elsewhere'.[11] Fijian leaders briefly mooted the idea of integration with Britain, but in 1964 a new legislative council was created with elected seats for fourteen Fijians, twelve Indians and ten Europeans. A member system began with three Fijian unofficial elected members given portfolios. After general elections in 1966, the high-born Ratu Kamisese Mara formed a ministry and in 1969 expressed willingness to accept Dominion status (now an archaic concept) provided there were safeguards for Fijians. A complex multi-member, tri-racial, electoral system was devised, giving equality between Fijians and Indians in the House of Representatives, with the settler minority holding the balance. Fiji became independent on 10 October 1970.[12]

The Kingdom of Tonga had preceded Fiji by five months. It had always been self-governing as a constitutional monarchy, with the British Agent only responsible for external affairs and defence, with powers of scrutinizing finances, legislation and appointments. Revisions to the Treaty of Friendship in 1958 and 1968 progressively removed the British powers, which appeared increasingly anachronistic after neighbouring Western Samoa became independent in 1962. Moreover, Tonga, along with Western Samoa and Fiji, was a founder-member of the Pacific Islands Producers Association in 1965, indicating its desire for taking more initiative in its own development. Tonga appointed a Commissioner in London in 1969 and celebrated full independence, the end of Protected State status, on 4 June 1970.[13]

Papua New Guinea, the most populous of the island states, with a population of 3 million, was not, of course, a British responsibility, being an Australian-administered UN Trust Territory. Its government remained colonial through the 1950s and attracted adverse comment in the UN. Elections were not held until 1964. Thereafter there was a gallop to self-government. A chief minister was appointed in 1973, and independence was conferred on 16 September 1975, with Australia agreeing to underwrite 40 per cent of the budget.

In the scattered islands of the Solomons and the Gilbert and Ellice groups, the problems of distance, transport, island particularism and economic underdevelopment had all been compounded by Japanese invasion in the 1939–45 war followed by an American occupation. In the Solomons, a protest movement known as Maasina Rule (meaning

'Brotherhood' but dubbed by the authorities 'Marching Rule' or 'Marxian Rule') created alternative institutions based on tradition, but was put down by force between 1947 and 1949. Constitutional advance was slow until an FCO minister visited in 1975, and a chief minister was appointed. Elections were held in 1977, and independence followed on 7 July 1978.[14] The story was somewhat similar in the Gilbert and Ellice Islands where the distances were even greater and the situation complicated by British nuclear tests at Christmas Island, US claims on some of the islands, controversy over Ocean Island (Banaba), and rivalry between Micronesian Gilbertese and Polynesian Ellice Islanders. The royalties from Ocean Island phosphates had long underpinned the colony's revenues, but this was a wasting asset, as in Nauru. The Banabans, who had been removed by the Japanese, had relocated after the war on Rabi Island in Fiji (bought with phosphate royalties), but they called for the separation of Banaba from the Gilberts. There was some talk of a Cook Islands solution for the colony. Anthony Kershaw, an FCO under-secretary, went in 1972 to make it clear that Britain wanted to give independence, only to find that the Ellice Islanders wanted separation from the Gilbert Islands. With memories of Anguilla still in mind, the authorities organized a referendum in 1974 and found that 92 per cent of the Ellice Islanders preferred separation. In 1975, they became Tuvalu (Eight Islands Together, population 7,200) and went on to independence on 1 October 1978. In Kiribati (pronounced Kiribass, for Gilberts) elections were held in 1978, and independence achieved on 10 July 1979.[15] With a population of 60,000, living on 33 islands, the new state covered two million square miles of ocean.

The last and hastiest withdrawal in the Pacific was from the New Hebrides where political development had been delayed by the Anglo-French Condominium system under which each power had jurisdiction over its own nationals, so that administration, such as it was, was duplicated. British officials called it the 'Pandemonium'. Of the 45,000 indigenous people, 80 per cent had come under the influence of English-speaking Protestant missions, but the 2,000 French and 4,000 French-speaking Vietnamese residents heavily outnumbered the 330 British subjects. British officials wanted either to unload the islands on to Australia or France, or to partition them to allow unified administration in the respective parts. Decolonization was delayed by lack of British–French agreement, land disputes between Europeans and the New Hebrideans, and secessionist movements in several islands. At the time of the first elections in 1975, an attempted secession by Espiritu Santo was encouraged by disaffected French *colons* and some American speculators looking for a free enterprise tax haven. The British had been eager to get out since the 1960s; the French were only converted by the National Party (Vanua'aku Pati) boycotting the assembly and elections in 1978 and declaring a People's Provisional Government. Then, the co-domini could agree, at last, to go. After a further election in 1979, a government was formed by Father Walter Lini as chief minister. Independence for Vanuatu (Our Land) was set for 30 July 1980, but had to be upheld by British and French marines who were rushed in at the last minute because of secession movements on three islands. Unity was eventually enforced by units of the Papua New Guinea defence force, flown in by the Australian air force.[16] Decolonization in Vanuatu was the nearest approach in the Pacific to a Palestine- or Aden-type scuttle.

In the other region of mini and micro states, the Caribbean, closing the files on imperial outposts was more straightforward than in the Pacific. The precedents had been set after the collapse of the West Indies Federation in 1962. The experiment of 'free association' had always been terminable. Moreover, in spite of the demise of the Federation and the failure to create one for the 'Little Eight' in the eastern Caribbean, some common services were maintained, namely the university (with campuses at Jamaica, Trinidad and Barbados), certain joint shipping, airline, and meteorological services. Ministerial meetings were held to manage these services and a willingness to co-operate bore fruit in the creation of the Caribbean Free Trade Area, CARIFTA, in 1968, and the Common Market, CARICOM, in 1973.[17] In these regional institutions, the independent states, Jamaica, Trinidad, Barbados and Guyana, co-operated with the smaller islands. It was in many ways logical, and unproblematical, when these chose to end Associate Statehood and opted for full independence, which occurred in Grenada (7 February 1974), Dominica (3 November 1978), St Lucia (22 February 1979), St Vincent (27 October 1979), Antigua (1 November 1981) and St Kitts–Nevis (18 September 1983).

Two further Caribbean colonies reached the same terminus via separate routes. The Bahamas, which had enjoyed representative government since the nineteenth century, moved to a ministerial system in 1964, and after general elections in 1967 and 1968, moved to full internal self-government. In 1972, the assembly voted in favour of independence; a constitutional conference was held in London, and independence was gained on 10 July 1973. In British Honduras, which had received elected representation in the 1930s, a member system began in 1955, followed by a ministerial system in 1961, and full self-government in 1964. But independence was delayed because of claims on the territory (which had adopted the name Belize in 1973) by neighbouring Guatemala. After independence was granted on 21 September 1981, a British garrison remained for thirteen years.

The final crisis of British decolonization was the Rhodesian issue. UDI had come as an unwelcome storm at the end of the 'Wind of Change', one which buffeted several British Governments and dogged the Commonwealth Secretariat for its first fifteen years. It was even said that Ian Smith did more than Arnold Smith to raise the Secretariat's profile. The white Rhodesians were able to hold out for so long for three reasons. South Africa gave help in breaking sanctions and providing some military aid; the flanks were covered by Portuguese-ruled territories, and there were serious divisions among the African nationalists. Federation had been opposed (as it had by the African leaders of the northern protectorates) by Joshua Nkomo, who headed the Southern Rhodesian African National Congress. After the Congress was banned during the 1959 security scare, Nkomo created the National Democratic Party in 1960, which was also banned, so he formed the Zimbabwe African People's Union, ZAPU, which was banned, in turn, in 1962. The movement then split and the more radical members, Ndabaningi Sithole and Robert Mugabe, founded the rival Zimbabwe African National Union, ZANU. With ZAPU and ZANU vying for support, sometimes using intimidation, the Rhodesian regime, as it pondered the possibility of UDI, banned both parties and detained most of the leaders, who languished in jail for ten years. Others went into exile in neighbouring Zambia, Tanzania or Mozambique. From 1966, occasional guerrilla raids were made into Rhodesia, while rival armies were built up among the exiles. Eventually, ZANU developed the Zimbabwe African National Liberation Army, ZANLA, with Chinese arms and training, and ZAPU built the Zimbabwe People's Revolutionary Army, ZIPRA, with East German and Russian help. In this way, Zimbabwe nationalists harnessed the Cold War for their own ends. These, and equivalent movements in Angola and Mozambique, accentuated anti-communist paranoia among the whites of Southern Africa. Until 1972, the guerrilla incursions were sporadic: thereafter a civil war developed which, by the end of the 1970s, was costing numerous lives, yet victory was not in sight for either side. Peace only came from outside pressure which gradually edged the parties to an agreed settlement.

     The first outside pressure came after the British Conservative election victory in 1970. In 1971, the Smith regime was persuaded by the British

Government to make some concessions in the direction of the five NIBMAR principles, and Lord Pearce headed a royal commission to see whether the changes were acceptable to Rhodesian opinion. To oppose this settlement, an African National Council was created under Bishop Abel Muzorewa (the established nationalist leaders being in detention or in exile). Higher paid Africans said 'Yes' to the settlement, but crowds everywhere held up placards with 'Big Big No' and Pearce's conclusion was negative.

Pressure came, next, from South Africa and Zambia, which, in different ways, were affected by the guerrilla war and persuaded Smith to meet with Muzorewa and draw up principles for a multi-racial polity in Rhodesia. The third, and crucial, pressure came in the wake of the collapse of the Portuguese empire. The Portuguese, like the French after the 1939–45 war, granted citizenship rights to the small educated élite who embraced European culture. From the 1960s they sought to suppress the nationalists in Guinea-Bissau, Angola and Mozambique by force. But in 1973 General Spinola had declared that the war in Guinea could not be won. Army officers mounted the coup in Lisbon in April 1974 which topped a forty-four-year dictatorship, paving the way for a democratic constitution and independence for Mozambique in July 1975 under the Front for the Liberation of Mozambique, FRELIMO. Suddenly, Rhodesia's long eastern frontier came under a regime hospitable to the Zimbabwe guerrillas. Then a fourth pressure came from the United States, increasingly alarmed at the appearance of Marxist regimes in Mozambique and also Angola, where Cuban troops were supporting the Movimento Popular de Libertação de Angola, MPLA. The Americans drew up a plan for Rhodesian independence in two years, while the British made preparations to implement it and tried negotiating with the parties. To forestall these moves, Smith made an agreement with Muzorewa in 1977 for an assembly of seventy-two African members and twenty-eight European members, and a ministerial council with equal numbers of each race. Elections were held in April 1979, and Muzorewa became prime minister of Zimbabwe–Rhodesia on 29 May 1979. As this followed very closely on the election of a Conservative government under Margaret Thatcher in Britain on 4 May, the world waited to see if Mrs Thatcher would recognize the Muzorewa Government as satisfying the requirement for majority rule.

By the late 1970s, decolonization was all but complete and the Commonwealth had become a mainly Third World forum. The final pressure for settlement in Rhodesia came from the Commonwealth and was exerted in four distinct ways. First, at the Lusaka CHOGM in August 1979, which had been preceded by a visit to Zambia, Malawi and Tanzania by the Queen (in spite of the war), pressure was put on Mrs Thatcher by the Australian prime minister, Malcolm Fraser, the Jamaican prime minister, Michael Manley, the conference host, Kenneth Kaunda, and also the FCO officials, to withhold recognition of the Smith/Muzorewa settlement and to summon a conference of all the parties, including the guerrilla leaders. Secondly, during the ensuing long, tortuous London conference between October and December 1979, the 'Front Line States', Zambia and Tanzania and also Mozambique, which were all suffering because of the war (partly through Rhodesian security forces incursions into, or bombing of, their territories), persuaded the Zimbabwe nationalist leaders to accept the British proposals. General Tongogara of ZANLA also played an influential role as he feared the guerrilla war was leading to disaster. The British gambled and made a final act of will. Before the settlement was signed, they sent a Governor to Rhodesia to rule by ordinance and prepare for general elections under universal suffrage. The agreed constitution provided for a parliamentary system, with reserved seats for whites, and also a Bill of Rights. A cease-fire was arranged for midnight 28 December 1979, at which point sanctions were lifted.

Thirdly, the cease-fire and assembly of belligerents was organized by a small Commonwealth Monitoring Force from Australia, Britain, Fiji, Kenya and New Zealand. Finally, a Commonwealth Observer Group was sent to report to heads of government as to whether there was a free and fair election. The polls were organized by British election supervisors, including some retired colonial governors and imperial history professors, and there were also 500 London policemen present. The result was an overwhelming victory for the ZANU leader, Robert Mugabe, who was called by the Governor to form a government. The Republic of Zimbabwe was recognized, finally, on 18 April 1980.[18] Mrs Thatcher failed to congratulate the victors, but her government left a British Military Advisory and Training Team, BMATT, to help integrate the Rhodesian Forces and the ZIPRA and ZANLA units into a national army.

The Zimbabwe elections provided a dramatic finale to the tortured drama of British decolonization in Africa which had begun with the Ghana election and Libyan independence in 1951. Ten years after Zimbabwe, Namibia became independent and became the Commonwealth's fiftieth member. But apart from the small enclave of Walvis Bay (which had been annexed to the Cape Colony), the country had never been a British dependency. This vast, sparsely populated, largely desert land, once German Southwest Africa, had been occupied by South Africa in the 1914–18 war, and had become a League of Nations Mandate, which South Africa refused to convert into a UN Trust Territory after the 1939–45 war. Various UN attempts through the International Court failed to persuade South Africa to grant self-determination and, in the mid-1960s, yet another guerrilla war was begun by the Southwest African People's Organization, SWAPO. In 1966, the UN voted to terminate the Mandate, but UN missions were denied entry by the South African rulers. A UN contact group (comprising Britain, Canada, France, the United States and West Germany) made an agreement with South Africa in 1978, setting out principles for self-rule, but for ten more years the guerrilla war continued, complicated by SWAPO's use of refuges in Angola, where the revolutionary forces were backed by Cuban arms. Not until the Cubans left Angola in 1988 was SWAPO allowed back into Namibia. UN-supervised elections were then held in 1989, and the independence of Namibia recognized on 21 March 1990, except for the Walvis Bay enclave which was still under South African sovereignty. This was, finally, released in 1994, a few months before the momentous general election in which Nelson Mandela and the African National Congress came to power. At this point South Africa returned to the Commonwealth after a thirty-three-year absence.

Part II

WHY DID THE BRITISH EMPIRE FALL?

The 'why' question is the most difficult one to answer. Did the Empire fall because of its size, complexity and contradictions? Was it a case of loss of nerve, or loss of interest by post-war Britain? Did the Empire become more a liability than an asset? Was it simply a case of ripe fruit falling from the tree? Should we, with Dennis Austin, invoke Gibbon: 'the causes of destruction multiplied with the extent of conquest', 'the stupendous fabric yielded to the pressure of its own weight'?[1] Or had the latter-day Rome simply outlived its usefulness, the tolerance of its subjects, and a balance of power which had permitted its existence?

In tackling the 'why' question historians are agreed that it needs to be viewed at three levels – metropolitan, global and colonial – but they differ widely in the emphasis which should be given to each. John Gallagher described the three elements as political growth overseas, domestic constraints in the metropolis, and international pressures.[2] Ronald Robinson pointed the finger more directly: to Indian nationalism, British social democracy and American anti-imperialism.[3] But, more recently, with Roger Louis, he admits to the difficulty of fathoming the balance between 'metropolitan infirmity, nationalist insurgency, and American or Soviet expansion'.[4] David Birmingham, addressing the question as to whether Africa's decolonization was the result of 'nationalist campaigning for independence, or … an imperial retreat, or … super power pressure to give access to a continent guarded by Europeans', gave the answer – 'all three …'[5] If these approaches are rather similar and cautious about according priority, Anthony Low is less reticent. Decolonization, he suggests, all but invariably required, first of all, 'the growth of nationalist sentiments and nationalist forces'. This was not the whole story, but international forces were rarely, he suggests, of great significance, while the imperial response was of prime significance.[6] John Darwin, summarizing the debate so far, in 1988, took the same three causes and sub-divided the metropolitan one. This indicated four explanations: first, political and social changes in the colonies leading to nationalism; secondly, decline of Britain's economic and military strength in relation to its commitment; thirdly, indifference to Empire within Britain and the development of a post-imperial economy; fourthly, new conditions in global politics after 1945, which made Empire obsolete.[7] More recently, he has labelled the groups of arguments as the 'domestic', 'international' and 'peripheral' theories.[8] Each of the three main explanations must be considered in turn.

7

THE METROPOLITAN DIMENSION

If the question is asked: 'What domestic pressures led the British to give up their Empire?', answers may be sought by considering politics and society, trade and finance, and government policy relating to Britain's position in the world.

A superficial look at British political traditions would indicate that imperialism had become associated with the Conservatives, and that decolonization was first of all a policy of the left. Yet the main phases of the 'When' discussion tend to belie this pattern. Dominion status had evolved before the Labour Party achieved prominence in British politics and the Statute of Westminster was enacted by a coalition government. Although Attlee's Government was responsible for South Asian decolonization, and the Wilson Government decided to complete the withdrawal from East-of-Suez, the Conservative Governments of 1951– 64, 1970–4 and 1979–97 sent more colonies to their independence and the big turning point was the 'Wind of Change' under Macmillan. There was, in fact, very little inter-party political debate about decolonization.

Stephen Howe, who made a detailed analysis of anti-colonialism on the left in British politics, concluded that 'Decolonisation was most of the time a remarkably marginal issue in British politics. Not one general election after 1918 featured the Empire as a major campaign issue . . . no party split on colonial questions either.'[1] David Goldsworthy examined colonial issues in British politics across the party spectrum and suggests, 'If the major parties are judged solely on the records of their leaders in office, it is not very apparent that there was any great contention between them over colonial issues.' It was only in terms of 'traditions, ideas, and self-images' that the parties differed. Labour had a radical, internationalist and liberationist stream vying with its liberal-humanitarians, both of which groups were 'anti-imperialist'. The

Conservatives had their imperialist, economic-unity traditionalists trying to restrain their moderate, liberal, realistic wing. But the influence of party feeling was 'latent and constraining rather than manifest and activist'.[2]

If pressure for decolonization cannot be found in party political debate, can it be found in underlying social and cultural trends? A. P. Thornton wrote, 'as the Welfare State began to live the Empire began to die'.[3] R. F. Holland also wondered if the end of the European empires stemmed from 'a progressive mentality' among the post-war middle classes which embraced the welfare state and social freedoms; 'one reason why colonies were hustled towards independence ... was precisely to release west European resources for domestic welfare spending'.[4] Yet, as John Darwin rejoined, the Attlee Government, which did so much for the welfare state, did not balk at military expenditure to maintain a great power role, nor at employing national service conscripts in colonial emergencies.[5] Thornton maintained that the British people themselves 'were always indifferent to the future of the British Empire'.[6]

Social arguments have also been mounted to explain Britain's decline in the world, and which might be related to decolonization. Martin Weiner and Corelli Barnett have argued that British culture, from the nineteenth century, was anti-business, anti-industry and anti-capitalist, as a result, mainly, of the public schools and ancient universities, where the education, they suggest, was non-scientific and non-technical and dominated by the study of classics. Hence, a romantically inclined, liberal-educated élite was ill-equipped to make rational choices about Britain's overall strategies. Thus, in *The Lost Victory*, Barnett argued that the Attlee Government pursued the twin illusions of 'Third World Power' and 'New Jerusalem'.[7] As against this 'cultural critique', W. D. Rubinstein suggests that

> Britain's high culture was, demonstrably, perhaps the least hostile to entrepreneurship and business life of any in Europe and perhaps in the world; its intellectuals were least alienated of those of any leading society; and that Britain's culture was becoming more rational and positivistic rather than less from 1850 onwards ... it seems arguable that British culture is far less anti-capitalist and far more sympathetic to business life and entrepreneurship than virtually any other national culture in the world ...

He found that comparison with Germany, the often-vaunted technologically educated rival, suggests that its middle classes, too, were also educated in the classics.[8]

*

Turning from politics, society and culture as determinants of
decolonization, we must confront the faltering British economy. As Paul
Kennedy wrote: 'there is a noticeable "lag time" between the trajectory
of a state's relative economic strength and the trajectory of its
military/territorial influence'.[9] The problem here, however, is that the
eclipse of the British economy in relation to its rivals came at the end of
decolonization, not before. There was, nevertheless, a close coincidence
between the main landmarks of decolonization and Britain's major
financial crises. But the relationship between them was different in each
case and decolonization decisions did not necessarily follow directly
from financial constraints.

In the depression of the early thirties, 1931 was the year when
unemployment reached 2.75 million (10 per cent) and Britain devalued
the pound and went off the gold standard. It was the year of the opening
of the Indian Round Table Conference and the Statute of Westminster,
both of which had their origins long before the crisis. And in 1932, the
preferential tariff arrangements and quota agreements hammered out
at the Ottawa Economic Conference were designed, as Neville
Chamberlain said, to 'bring the Empire together again'.[10] Another
severe financial crisis attended the end of the 1939–45 war and it dogged
the days of the Attlee Government. One week after Japan's surrender –
even before the formal ceremonies in Tokyo Bay – President Truman
ended Lend-Lease on 21 August, inducing what Lord Keynes called a
'financial Dunkirk'.[11] As well as being kept going since 1942 by American
Lend-Lease, Britain had run up debts to the Empire in the form of
'sterling balances', which amounted to over £1 billion to India alone and
another £400 million to Egypt and Sudan. Annual military expenditure
was running at £725 million. To meet immediate import needs, as
industry reverted to peace-time manufacturing, the Government sent
Keynes to seek an American grant or interest-free loan of $5 billion. It was
not forthcoming, but Britain could borrow $3.75 billion from the US,
with the balance made up to the $5 billion by another loan from Canada.
At the time of the Victory Parade in June 1946, as American soldiers
led the march past, their Congress had not yet ratified the dollar loan.

This financial Dunkirk had no immediate impact on decolonization.
The idea that Britain should give the Americans the island of Tarawa in
the Gilbert Islands for a war memorial and as a sweetener for the loan
was firmly rejected by Attlee. But one of the conditions of the loan was
that sterling should be made freely convertible within a year and there
was another severe crisis at the moment of convertibility, in July 1947,

on the eve of the ending of the Raj. This phase of decolonization reached a crucial watershed in late 1946 and early 1947, in an atmosphere of undoubtedly dire economic circumstances. The decisions about withdrawal from India, Burma, Ceylon and Palestine and the ending of aid to Greece were made during the worst winter in memory, including the fuel crisis in February 1947, when British factories had to close for three weeks, badly damaging the export drive. As a result of the financial crisis of July 1947, convertibility was cancelled in August, and the pound was devalued in 1949. While the decolonization decisions of early 1947 had long-standing origins and were designed to cut losses so that British power and influence could be maintained elsewhere, financial constraints were a continuing background anxiety. But they were not insuperable. During the Korean War, in 1950, a massive rearmament programme was begun, defence expenditure more than doubled and conscription was increased to two years. The position of Britain as a great power was, indeed, reasserted in the 1940s and 1950s at considerable cost to the domestic economy.

A third serious financial crisis occurred in 1956 at the time of Suez. The US refused dollars and oil until a cease-fire was agreed and Macmillan, who had been 'first in, first out',[12] was soon calling for his 'profit and loss account' of colonies approaching self-government. Here, again, a direct connection with decolonization is not clear. The decision on independence for the Sudan, Ghana and Malaya had been made *before* the Suez crisis and the profit and loss report proved indecisive. The balance was seen as 'evenly matched' and withdrawal from unprofitable but inexpensive colonies would be regarded as 'discreditable'.[13] The 'Wind of Change' depended more on events in Africa and dramatic changes in French and Belgian policy.

By contrast with the 'Wind of Change', the withdrawal from East-of-Suez can be linked more closely with financial crisis. Harold Wilson's Government began by upholding an East-of-Suez policy. The Healey defence review was concerned with rationalizing commitments and had the windfall of the end of Indonesian Confrontation to build on. But the devaluation crisis of November 1967 and the expenditure cuts of early 1968 had their impact on the decision to withdraw from the Singapore base and from Aden and the Gulf States. By the next major financial crisis of 1976, when Britain had to seek a $3.9 billion IMF loan – the largest yet granted – and was required to cut £4 billion from government expenditure as a condition, decolonization was all but completed. Historians have not, as yet, tried to connect withdrawal from the last Pacific colonies to the IMF-induced economies.

It is also hard to link decolonization directly to Britain's changing position as a trading nation. At the peak of its strength as the most powerful empire and 'workshop of the world' in the Victorian era of free trade, around the 1860s, Britain was a global, not simply a colonial, trader. The Empire accounted for about a quarter of its overseas trade. On the eve of the 1914–18 war, the Empire supplied only about 20 per cent of imports and took 22 per cent of exports. But the siege mentality induced by the war gave encouragement to those who had been calling for a protected imperial trading system. After some moves were made in this direction by the Ottawa Agreements of 1932, the Empire began to have a bigger role. By 1936, it supplied nearly 40 per cent of imports and took nearly half Britain's exports. Further distortions of trading patterns caused by the 1939–45 war accentuated the value of Empire/ Commonwealth, especially through the bulk purchase agreements made with Empire suppliers. By the end of the war the all-time peak of intra-imperial trade was reached.

Around 1950, for the first and only time, over half British exports went to Empire markets. Thus, in spite of the financial Dunkirk and dollar loans, the imperial economic system seemed to be serving Britain well at a time when Germany and Japan were devastated by the war. In 1951, British industrial production exceeded that of Germany and France combined, and British exports exceeded those of France, Germany and Japan combined. But as Germany, Japan and the Western European states rebuilt their economies with generous American help, the Empire/Commonwealth markets grew more slowly. By 1961, British exports to Western Europe were as great as those to the Commonwealth and by 1967, exports to the original six of the EEC alone exceeded exports to the Commonwealth, which continued its relative decline as a market for British goods. By 1980, over half Britain's trade was with Europe generally and only 12 per cent with the Commonwealth. The British share of world manufactures, which in 1950 had been 25 per cent, was down to 10 per cent in 1970.[14] By the 1980s, Germany's manufacturing production was three times that of Britain and France's was double.[15] The 1960s to 1980s were the years of collapse for Britain's relative industrial and trading position. It helps explain the applications to join the EEC in 1961 and 1967, and the resumption of negotiations in 1969, culminating in entry by 1973. These events coincided with, but cannot be seen as the causes of, rapid decolonization.

In seeking the domestic pressures for decolonization, we are left with considerations of policy-making and Britain's view of her role in the world. This leads to the paradoxical conclusion that Britain moved out of the Empire to maintain her position as a world power. Even as the Attlee Government dismantled the South Asian Empire in 1947–8, it was seeking to bolster British influence in Western Europe, the Middle East, Africa and Southeast Asia. While remaining aloof from ideas about, and the movement towards, integrating Western Europe politically and economically, the Labour Government fostered defence co-operation through the Dunkirk Treaty with France (1947), the Brussels Pact (1948), and Nato (1949). Militarily, Britain continued to behave as a great power and was able to invoke aid from the Dominions, as in the Berlin airlift, 1948–9, when air crews from Australia and New Zealand (but not Canada) gave assistance.

In the Middle East, Britain held, as we have seen, unprecedented sway from Tripoli to Tehran and from Cyprus to Somaliland at the end of the 1939–45 war. When Palestine became an incurable cancer, requiring ever-costly therapy, the Mandate was abandoned in 1948 in the interests of good relations with the Arab states. Here, Ernest Bevin hoped to relate to 'peoples not pashas' and envisaged welfare reforms under British tutelage with the Middle East states co-operating in a regional defence organization. As Roger Louis has put it: 'Non-intervention thus becomes intervention by other means.'[16] Bevin's stance on the Middle East was Palmerstonian in its grandeur. When Attlee, in 1946, questioned the need for maintaining Britain's position in such 'deficit areas' and mooted an accord with the Soviet Union (which he believed was fearful of its southern flank), he provoked a threat of resignation by the Chiefs of Staff, which Bevin supported. The Middle East housed, as well as the Suez Canal and the Gulf oilfields, air bases for launching strategic bombing raids on the Soviet Union. The region was deemed to be vital for defence, so Attlee (who got his way over India) gave way over the Middle East. British strategy until the mid-1950s was obsessed with contingency planning to deny the Middle East to the Soviet Union in the event of a third world war. In this endeavour, support was sought from Canada, Australia, New Zealand, South Africa and Southern Rhodesia. New Zealand showed willing from 1948; Australia made some less categorical commitments. Australian air units went to Malta and a New Zealand squadron went to Cyprus in the early 1950s. Attlee agreed with Bevin about a British bomb. In 1946 Bevin insisted: 'We've got to have this thing over here, whatever it costs ... We've got to have a bloody Union Jack flying on top of it.'[17] It took time to develop, but Britain tested the A-Bomb at the Monte Bello Islands and Maralinga in Australia in 1952–7, and an H-Bomb at Christmas Island in the Gilberts in 1957–8.

The Labour Government dreamt of developing the African Empire as a substitute for India. Africa would provide food for Britain and Bevin said that, in minerals, 'we could have the United States dependent on us, and eating out of our hand in four or five years'.[18] In Southeast Asia, where, as Bevin told the 1946 PMM, the Empire was 'somewhat strung out',[19] the new Commissioner-General was sent out by the Foreign Office in 1946 to co-ordinate British relations with Burma, Thailand, French Indo-China and the Netherlands East Indies. In the same year, the Colonial Office sent a Governor-General to take an overview of the medley of colonies and protected states in Singapore, Malaya and Borneo. Bevin envisaged a wide and continuing British influence – the campaign against communist insurgents in Malaya from 1948, the ANZAM Arrangements (a planning system for Australia, New Zealand and the Malayan area) from 1949, and the Colombo Plan, from 1950–1, were all designed to foster stability in the region, and protect British investments (especially in Malaya's rubber and tin) and strategic interests.

Decolonization in this context was designed to secure co-operation with sympathetic local élites, who would facilitate development and be susceptible to continuing British influence and trade. Britain would remain a world power, a worthy ally to the United States in the Cold War. As Darwin put it: 'Colonial rule must die that influence might live; empire must be sacrificed to world power.'[20] Gallagher suggested that as imperialism became obsolete, Britain reverted to nineteenth-century methods of informal empire. Louis and Robinson have argued that 'The formal Empire contracted in the post-war years as it had once expanded, as a variable function of integrating countries into the international capitalist economy.'[21] Nicholas Tarling expressed the same theme in political terms: 'Britain was following through a concept already formulated in the nineteenth century, that of a world of states the relationships among which were economic and diplomatic rather than territorial and imperial.' It was a case, he suggests, of 'adaptation rather than abandonment ...' 'The merely imperial stage ... was over.'[22]

The same trend in respect of finance and the City was traced by Peter Cain and Anthony Hopkins, in their wide-ranging linking of British imperialism to domestic history. They developed the concept of 'gentlemanly capitalism' – a combination of landed wealth with banking and commercial expertise which had made the City of London the most dynamic element of the British economy – a development which, they say, predated and outlived Britain's brief period as 'workshop of the world'. After British manufactures became less competitive in the later nineteenth century, the services of the City continued to expand up to the 1914–18 war. Between the wars, when the City's declining ability to lend began to circumscribe its influence, a sterling bloc, later the sterling area, was created to maintain the City's role by pooling gold and dollar resources. In the 1950s, however, because of Britain's post-war indebtedness and the faster recovery of the other industrialized nations, it became clear that Empire, Commonwealth and sterling area were all too confined as a sphere of primary operation. The City, therefore, turned to a wider post-imperial role as provider of financial services to economies more successful than Britain's.[23]

In the long run, these reversions to non-imperial modes of maintaining power and influence failed. Financial constraints forced an eventual reduction of military power after nearly three decades of overspending on defence at a time when industrial rivals such as Germany and Japan spent comparatively little. But there were also global reasons for Britain's relative decline as a power, which now must be addressed.

8

THE GLOBAL DIMENSION

While there is disagreement about the nature and significance of the metropolitan dimension of decolonization, there is less cause for doubt about the general outlines of the changing international environment. Germany had been eliminated as a colonial rival in the 1914–18 war, and schemes for its colonial 'restitution' in the 1930s made no headway. However, Italy's incursion into Ethiopia excited anti-imperialist feelings in many parts of Africa, and Japan's expansion into Asia and the Pacific gave new opportunities for some nationalists in Burma, Malaya and India. In helping to defeat the German, Italian and Japanese bids for regional hegemony, the British protected or recovered their colonies, but the Empire was severely tested and weakened by the 1939–45 war.

Ideologically, imperialism had long been under international challenge. In this respect the outcome of the 1914–18 war marked a major watershed. In 1917, the Bolshevik Revolution and Woodrow Wilson's Fourteen Points had provided rival blueprints for a new world order which altered, forever, the context of colonial rule. Thus, territorial imperialism, as practised by Italy and Japan in the 1930s, had become unacceptable. The League of Nations and the Mandate system had injected, however fitfully, the notion of international accountability for colonial rule. The idea of 'Dual Mandate' envisaged development for the joint benefit of ruler and ruled. Eventual self-rule was envisaged for much of the Empire beyond the Dominions and some advances were already in train in Indian provinces, Egypt, Ceylon and the West Indies. By the 1930s, J. M. Bonn was writing of the era of 'counter-colonization and decolonization'. Anti-imperialism was espoused by myriad groups on the left of British politics but also, more influentially, by many Americans. It was American anti-imperialism which prompted much of the rethinking of colonial goals in Whitehall during the 1939–45 war.

There was a realization that American capital resources would be needed to prompt the development necessary to raise living standards. During the war, however, Churchill resented such anti-imperialist pressures.

When the publication of the Atlantic Charter, in August 1941, excited nationalists in many quarters, Churchill told his Cabinet that the aims set forth in the Charter did not apply to the colonial Empire. It was 'directed to the nations of Europe whom we hoped to free from Nazi tyranny, and was not intended to deal with the internal affairs of the British Empire'.[1] The British Government had already made pledges about Indian and colonial self-government. But after the Japanese had been checked in the Pacific, by mid-1942, and on the eve of the British–American landings in North Africa, *Life* magazine published an 'Open Letter to the People of England' on 12 October 1942, which insisted: 'one thing we are sure we are *not* fighting for is to hold the British Empire together ... Our side is plenty big ... It is much bigger than the British Raj'.[2] Churchill made his position clear in a Mansion House speech on 10 November 1942, when he hailed the American involvement in fighting the Germans in Africa. 'We mean to hold our own. I have not become the King's First Minister in order to preside over the liquidation of the British Empire.'[3] In 1944 he wrote: ' "Hands off the British Empire" is our maxim and it must not be weakened or smirched to please sob-stuff merchants at home or foreigners of any hue.'[4] At the Yalta Conference with Roosevelt and Stalin in February 1945, he misinterpreted the import of a discussion on the trusteeship issue, which was supposed to focus on the League of Nations mandates and the ex-enemy colonies. He exclaimed: 'I will have no suggestion that the British Empire is to be put in the dock and examined by everyone to see whether it is up to their standard.'[5] But at the San Francisco Conference on the UN organization in 1945, the trusteeship discussions found Australia and New Zealand ganging up with the US against the colonial powers. In the Trusteeship Council, the UN provided a new forum for anti-colonialist expression and pressures.

The onset of the Cold War in the late 1940s brought a paradoxical impact. On the one hand, American anti-imperialism became muted as the US turned to prop up, and ease the passing of, the British Empire for American strategic reasons. On the other hand, the Cold War provided new opportunities for anti-colonial movements and gave colonial nationalists new ideologies to deploy, and it provided new sources of material aid for freedom fighters. As well as marking the pervasive background to the era of decolonization, the Cold War was invoked in explicit ways, which had a considerable effect on the timing of decolonization in certain areas.

A foretaste was evident at the 1946 Prime Ministers' Meetings when the British Chiefs of Staff presented their first post-war strategic appreciation, which envisaged the Soviet Union as the only potential enemy and saw a third world war beginning with possible Soviet incursions into Western Europe and the Middle East. For the next twenty years, all British strategic appreciations were dominated by the Soviet threat and the resources, bases and forces of the Empire/Commonwealth were always brought into the calculations. Thus, each PMM began with a *tour d'horizon* exposition of the state of the Cold War, which was not always appreciated by the leaders of newly independent states. When the special constitutional conference, called in 1949 to settle the issue of India as a republic, degenerated into a minor squabble about fulfilling defence obligations in the Cold War, Nehru deprecated the concentration of an old Dominion, like New Zealand, on defence issues.[6] He preferred to alleviate the conditions which made communism attractive. Similarly, at the 1964 PMM, which brought forth the proposals for the Commonwealth Secretariat and the Foundation, Nkrumah deplored the fact that they spent the first day discussing communism. He wanted the Cold War kept out of Commonwealth discussions. However, in region after region, as the Cold War expanded, it could not be avoided in the decolonization debates.

It first affected the Middle East, where the British clung to their bases because of their strategic potential for bombing the Soviet Union. Nasser's acceptance of military aid from the communist bloc prompted the withdrawal of funds for the Aswan Dam, which led to the Suez crisis. Soviet influence, through the Egyptian teachers in Somalia and the Sudan, was seen as a potential threat to East Africa.

The most explicit impact of the Cold War, of course, came in Malaya with the outbreak of the communist insurrection in 1948. It is significant that when, soon after this, Nkrumah organized his radical CPP in the Gold Coast, there were immediate moves to expose his earlier links with the British Communist Party and attempts to find communist influences in the Gold Coast. The new governor, Arden-Clarke, had experience in anti-communist security techniques used in Southeast Asia.[7] In both Malaya and the Gold Coast, the British accepted that they had to win the support of moderates in order to pre-empt potential extremists. In the Malayan case, Britain also supplied security forces in the Far East Strategic Reserve and participated in the Manila Pact and Seato in the wake of China's intervention in the Korean War in 1950. In face of fears that China might interfere, again, to assist local communist movements in Southeast Asia, Britain's decolonization in Malaya was accompanied by security guarantees and force deployments in co-operation with Australia and New Zealand.

Another area of explicit fear of communism was British Guiana. Documents listing the Marxian connections of Dr Jagan and his ministers were circulated to the British Cabinet in 1953, and the self-government constitution was suspended after only a few months. When Britain resumed decolonization in Guiana in the 1960s, it was against the background of Fidel Castro's coming to power in the Cuban revolution of 1959. There was pressure from the United States to go slow in Guiana, but the British went ahead; the colony became independent in 1966 and four years later became the Co-operative Republic of Guyana.[8]

The Castro bogey was also invoked in Southeast Asia and the Pacific. The Malayan Emergency formally ended in 1960, at a moment when there was a swing to the left in Singapore politics which saw Lee Kuan Yew's PAP lose two by-elections. Fears that Singapore would become a 'second Cuba' lay behind Tengku Abdul Rahman's moves towards merger and Malaysia.[9] Also at this time, the slow political development of the Pacific Islands prompted comments that this region was becoming the last bastion of colonialism. As Soviet diplomats courted island representatives at international gatherings, Britain's Commissioner-General in Singapore feared the 'Cold War front is advancing upon Oceania'.[10] Tensions between Indians and Fijians prompted a New Zealand fear that Fiji could be yet another 'potential Cuba'.[11] The same was said of Zanzibar in 1964, after a supposedly Cuban-supported revolt ousted the Sultan of Zanzibar a few months after independence.

The final area of Cold War impact was in Central Africa. Nationalists in the Portuguese colonies of Angola and Mozambique, and the rival groups in Rhodesia, looked for assistance, arms and training to the Soviet Union, East Germany, Cuba or China in the 1970s. The Zimbabwe nationalists were able to exploit Cold War tensions for their own ends. At the same time, the Rhodesian, South African and British Governments became more adamant in their unwillingness to negotiate with what they dubbed 'communist terrorists'. And because of the extension of the Cold War into Central and Southern Africa, American intervention became an element to be taken into account in the settlement in Zimbabwe.[12]

The Cold War, then, was part of the global backdrop to decolonization, but only a part. The pace of change could be affected, in more explicit ways, by events in former rival empires. Decolonization by other powers induced, in some cases, a snowball effect. The ending of the Raj, in 1947, was the fulfilment of decisions made in the 1930s and promises confirmed during the war. It did not stem primarily from international pressures, but it was not the first landmark of colonial devolution. The Philippines had been given self-government by the United States in the 1930s and gained their formal independence on 4 July 1946. The ending of the Palestine Mandate, however, was heavily influenced by pressures from the US and the UN, as well as by the terrorist movements within the territory and by domestic frustration in Britain about performing a thankless task. The decision to grant independence to Ghana and Nigeria was little influenced by outside pressures. Indeed, South Africa's attitude induced great caution in Britain's public admission and presentation of its decisions, if not its intentions. At the same time, the British position in Malaya and Borneo could be pictured as increasingly anachronistic against the background of the ending of the Raj, independence in the Philippines, the Dutch departure from Indonesia in 1949, the creation of the Peoples' Republic of China in the same year, and France's collapse in Indo-China in 1954. Shortly before his first election victory, Tengku Abdul Rahman attended the Bandung Conference. By the time of Malayan independence in 1957, Britain's Borneo colonies were the last European dependencies in Southeast Asia except Dutch West New Guinea and Portuguese East Timor.

The 'Wind of Change' must also be viewed against the global background. It did not stem immediately from Macmillan's profit and loss analysis, but it was certainly part of the post-Suez realization of Britain's inability to act as an independent power and it was also affected by Cold War anxieties. American fears about a spread of Soviet influence in Africa led to a high-level official enquiry on 'Africa: the Next Ten Years', which took place in 1959, the year of Castro's victory and of unusual political passion in Britain about Kenya and Nyasaland.[13] Macleod grasped the nettle early in 1960, but events in the Congo and Algeria caused him to increase the pace. In 1960, seventeen new countries joined the UN, all but two of which were in Africa. While the 'Wind of Change' blew itself out in Africa, Macmillan turned to persuade his colleagues that Britain's future lay in Europe and made the first application to enter the EEC in 1961. Finally, in 1979, the last major watershed of decolonization – the breaking of the Rhodesia–Zimbabwe deadlock – depended on the Portuguese coup of 1974, and the independence of Mozambique and Angola in 1975, which exposed the flank of the secessionist regime in Rhodesia. This, along with the growing American interest in Southern African affairs, helped to force the parties to the negotiating table.

The impact of the global dimension on decolonization, then, was to evoke a progressive, though somewhat uneven and fitful, realization of Britain's inability to maintain the independent stance of a great power. In the global confrontation between the super powers, Britain was only influential in concert with the United States, and after Suez, Macmillan explicably accepted the role of junior partner in the alliance. Louis and Robinson suggest that the 'strategic significance of pan-Arabism, of pan-Africanism, and of the non-aligned nations in the cold war motivated the final dismantling of formal empire'.[14]

In the colonial territories, Britain's interests had now to be fostered by some post-colonial means, which meant, in effect, re-exploring well-tried, pre-colonial pathways. Gallagher summed up the history of British imperialism as 'a system predominantly of influence turning into a system predominantly of rule and trying, unsuccessfully, to return to influence'.[15] But by the 1960s, it was too late. Britain had to choose between global ambitions, which it still cherished, and the possibility of a more prosperous and secure future in Europe. In the 1970s it chose the latter. Low has insisted that Britain's 'contraction' did not stem from loss of nerve. In the most succinct and suggestive one-sentence summary of the resolution of the dilemma, he suggested it was 'the entirely to be expected contraction of the all-too-overstretched dominion of a none-too-large and very distant island brought about . . . by the nemesis of normalcy'.[16]

9

THE COLONIAL DIMENSION

On the colonial dimension of decolonization there is least agreement among historians. It is, therefore, necessary to consider the role of what is called colonial 'nationalism', but which in many cases should perhaps be described as the independence-seeking coalitions. It is agreed that British policy-makers always underestimated the force of nationalism, and almost invariably found their timetables overtaken by events and the fear of disorder. It is also agreed that once Asian or African nationalists managed to build mass movements, they became irresistible. As Cain and Hopkins put it, 'nationalist aspirations could not be contained at a price that was worth paying, or perhaps at any price'.[1] But here agreement ends.

There are those who discount the role of colonial nationalism, especially in getting decolonization under way in Africa. Ronald Robinson wrote: 'Whatever persuaded the British empire in 1947 to plan its own demise in tropical Africa, it was not fear of black African freedom fighters.' Rather, he suggests that the Colonial Office's policies of development and gradual self-government (which he had helped to formulate) did more 'wittingly or unwittingly, to bring about the dismantling of British colonial rule and the rise of nationalism ... than most African politicians'.[2] The idea in the Colonial Office in the late 1940s, with which Sir Sidney Caine and Sir Andrew Cohen were particularly associated, was to cultivate colonial élites whose co-operation would be essential in the process of development. Thus, Robinson asks a famous question: was nationalism the 'continuation of imperialism by other and more efficient means?'[3] But the needs of development unleashed what Africans came to see as the 'second colonial occupation', as capital and experts (and in some cases settlers) came to the colonies. These incursions, in turn, stoked up long-simmering nationalist fires. Low gives greatest emphasis to the role of colonial nationalism and writes, 'It has lately been suggested that international pressures and domestic constraints were at least as important as colonial pressures ... This now seems scarcely tenable.' The 'Wind of Change' after 1959, he said, stemmed from 'above all the fervour in the nationalisms they were still confronting'. If it had not been for this, the Macmillan Government would not have moved so fast. 'Wherever one looks', says Low, 'nationalist upheavals against imperial rule set the pace'.[4]

The growth of colonial nationalism (however complex and fragile its political instruments) should be accorded a high place in explanations of the decolonization process. Whether it was generated by the earlier spread of education and ideas, or by the pioneering of the Dominions, or by the new interventionist policies after the 1939–45 war, or by the tenacity and renaissance of indigenous traditions and cultures, the so-called nationalist movements – the 'ramshackle' or 'gimcrack' coalitions as they were dubbed by Anil Seal[5] – were the driving force in the acceleration of decolonization in most cases. In India the process was worked out over the largest territorial span and over the longest timescale. The 'collaborators' identified by Gallagher and Robinson and their disciples were, in India, of long standing and existed at many levels. Thus, suggested Seal, the study of nationalism meant identifying 'the forces that drove Indian politics upwards and outwards from the oddities of the locality, or downwards from the hollow generalities of all-India'. Colonial nationalisms generally were made up of 'disparate aspirations and grievances ... somehow generalized into unities stronger than their own contradictions'.[6] As imperial rulers stretched deeper into colonial societies by creating local, provincial and territorial representative institutions, small power-brokers who were local bigwigs linked their own concerns to territory-wide agitations. 'Imperialism built a system which interlocked its rule in locality, province and nation; nationalism emerged as a matching structure of politics.'[7] And as Low reminded us, most of the colonial peoples were rural and lived in local communities dominated by various types of big-wig – communities which predated and outlived the phase of colonial rule. The territory-wide coalitions – the so-called 'nationalist movements' – to which the British transferred power, provided the political structures which endeavoured to rule the post-colonial states. Low has suggested that there were only half a dozen ways in which these coalitions arose. These were: 'natural majorities' based on a core community; 'composed majorities' in which several major communities combined; 'Prussians' or a cohesive group using muscle to gain predominance; the 'interstitial role' of a respected leader from a minority community; the 'primus inter pares option' where a number of equal regions existed; or the '50:50 system' where there were two evenly balanced communities.[8] This range of options gives some indication of the sort of forces which could lie behind colonial nationalism and sustain the coalitions to which power was transferred. Impressive façades of unity were sometimes displayed in the short run.

Dennis Austin has pointed out that although the British had always contemplated going – and often said they would – in the end they always had to be pushed.[9] The exceptions were in North Borneo, the Pacific Islands and the Arabian/Persian Gulf, where the British did the pushing. That is not to say that colonial nationalists 'drove out the colonialists' or even 'grasped power to themselves'. As the discussion of the 'How' question which follows will indicate, the British managed to evolve some well-tried procedures and they sought to transfer power, in an orderly fashion, to democratically elected successors. At least one general election (preferably more) was held to determine who had a mandate to rule. But in many cases, the results represented a disappointment of British intentions. The winners were not always those whom the British wanted, and actions after independence often fell short of British expectations.

The real impact of the colonial dimension to decolonization was the force of local events in pushing the British to their final decisions, however reluctantly they were made. Each case was different. Yet decisions in one region provided precedents for others; events in one colony had a snowball effect elsewhere.

The initiative in evolving the Dominion model had come from the old colonies. In the evolution of responsible government colonial ministers had come into conflicts with Governors over the minutiae of imperial reserve powers. If an issue was made, it was usually resolved in favour of colonial autonomy. The special designation 'Dominions' had been requested by the self-governing colonies themselves. The pushing of Dominion status to the outcome of full sovereignty was done on the initiative of the Canadians, the Irish and the South Africans. The British professed themselves pleased with the 'Statute of Westminster Commonwealth', but it had not been their idea.

At the end of the 1939–45 war, the Attlee Government came to power determined to fulfil the wartime pledges to give self-government in South Asia, and to prepare the rest of the Empire for economic development and gradual political advance. But they also intended to maintain Britain's position as a great power and saw Empire and Commonwealth having an important role in this. Their aim in India was a united federal regime in the sub-continent, but by the end of 1946, with Jinnah implacable in his demand for Pakistan, and Nehru insistent on a strong central government, Attlee suggested to his Cabinet colleagues that the ultimate result of Congress's policy would be the establishment of the very Pakistan which it did not want. But 'one thing was quite certain', said Attlee, '... we could not put back the clock'. The India and Burma Committee came to the conclusion 'that the pressure of events was leading towards the establishment of some form of Pakistan'.[10] Mountbatten soon came to the same conclusion. He hoped for an Indian Union with a strong central government, or failing that, with a weak centre. But after his meetings with Jinnah he realized that the force of Muslim nationalism was making the separation of India and Pakistan unavoidable. As he said on 11 April 1947, 'Everyone must bear in mind that the sheer logic of events and mechanical difficulties were likely to wield the greatest influence.'[11] It had been a similar story in Burma, which was regarded as a much less significant dependency. In 1946, as Governor Rance attempted to negotiate with Burmese nationalist groups, the prospect of agreement seemed slight. As Hugh Tinker wrote: 'events were now in control'.[12]

The same was true of the other retreats of the Attlee Government. Carefully considered Colonial Office plans for a gradual move to Dominion status for Ceylon, for a bi-national state in Palestine, for the Malayan Union, and for evolution to democratic government starting at the grassroots level in West Africa were all overtaken by the rising tide of nationalist agitation. The Ceylon Order-in-Council of 1946 was followed by strikes and riots. The Palestine Mandate became unworkable. The British Government refused to use force to impose a settlement which neither Jews nor Arabs accepted; the Mandate was simply given up. The Malay rulers refused to co-operate with Malayan Union and its chief architect decided, within weeks, that it was unworkable. Ideas about gradual education in democratic government in Africa, which Andrew Cohen thought would take a generation, were shattered by the 1948 riots in the Gold Coast and the emergence of Nkrumah.

This meant that the changes which these events induced in Malaya and the Gold Coast could not be halted by the Conservatives, who returned to power under Churchill in 1951. Although the new government went ahead with the white-dominated Central African Federation, and hoped to keep the Gold Coast from full Commonwealth membership, both the Gold Coast and Malaya went on to independence with membership in 1957, while Nigeria was set on the same path.

It might seem that Macmillan had the opportunity of a brief respite when he took office in 1957, but in the post-Suez period both the metropolitan and global environments had changed. Colonial affairs had to be viewed in a new context and, although Macmillan's profit and loss exercise was inconclusive, the 'logic of events' could not be avoided by 1959–60, because of the Kenya and Nyasaland crises, the sudden French and Belgian decolonizations, and mounting UN pressures. Moreover, dangerous African unrest in East and Central Africa and the mass support mobilized by Nyerere, Kenyatta, Banda and Kaunda were such that real fears of violence and bloodshed impelled Macleod to move even faster than Macmillan wanted. Thus it came about that the Macmillan and Douglas-Home Conservative Governments were responsible for the watershed decisions in Britain's decolonization. By the time of Wilson's withdrawal from East-of-Suez, Britain's financial weakness and its European orientation had become more influential than nationalist agitation in the withdrawal from the remaining colonies. In the case of Aden, however, decades of neglect and lack of policy could not be repaired by federalizing incompatible areas like the Aden Colony and the South Arabian Sheikhdoms. The ideological disputes of rival South Arabian groups proved so irreconcilable and violent that Britain simply pulled out without the normal transfer of power.[13] It was a final, messy, example of how rival ideologies and rising 'nationalist' fervour could produce a tense and untenable situation like the one Mountbatten labelled the 'logic of events'.

Unrest, and the fear of violence, always were powerful catalysts. Although British governments made recourse to military force in numerous emergencies of decolonization – in India, Palestine, Egypt, Cyprus, the Gold Coast, British Guiana, Kenya and Malaya – they did not cherish policies of repression. The five major accelerations noted in Part I of this book were each in part occasioned by fears of growing disorder with the possibility of widespread chaos. In 1947 Mountbatten advanced the timetable for partition because he feared the British might not be able to hold on. In 1951 Arden-Clarke gambled on Nkrumah to hold together the Gold Coast for gradual advance. In 1960 Macleod realized that he could not hold down the lid in East and Central Africa, especially after the French and Belgian about-turns and the ugly war in Algeria. If Wilson's 1968 withdrawal from East-of-Suez began as an economy measure, it was hastened by the breakdown in Aden. Finally, the 1980 settlement became possible in Zimbabwe because the sudden departure of the Portuguese from Africa had made the UDI regime vulnerable and the guerrilla war had become too costly for the Rhodesians, the Zimbabwean nationalists and the Front Line States.

Part III

How did the British Empire fall?

The 'how' question appears the most puzzling one to answer and, in many respects, the most neglected. It involves elaboration on what Low dubbed the 'old stately three-stage progression' from Crown colony, through representative and responsible government to Dominion status and sovereignty.[1] This process is not always understood clearly, and it reveals the interesting problem of Britain's extreme reluctance and delay in allowing many dependencies to reach the end of the route. There was reluctance to admit all but the select few to Dominion status. Then, no sooner was this granted, than the whole concept was mysteriously discarded. There was also reluctance to allow full and equal membership of the Commonwealth and, when this was finally conceded, the Commonwealth was, in the nature of things, completely transformed.

Dominion status and Commonwealth membership are, therefore, vital to an understanding of decolonization but, since the end-of-Empire happened, they have become unfashionable subjects, neglected by historians. Yet there is agreement that they gave British decolonization its unique flavour. Nicholas Mansergh suggested Britain's response to decolonization was 'individual and it was conditioned by ideas and by history'.[2] John Darwin wrote that the manner of its passing was 'not the least of the legacies of empire',[3] and David Reynolds admitted that Britain's retreat from Empire was 'distinctive'.[4]

In the years from 1915 to 1945, the 'British Commonwealth of Nations' was the élite club within the Empire. The members – Canada, Australia, New Zealand, South Africa, Newfoundland and the Irish Free State/Eire – became as politically independent as they wanted to be, but remained variously tied to Britain by the Crown, trade, finance, defence, migration, sentiment, sport and culture. This system was idealized, in 1937, by Sir Keith Hancock, who saw it as the resolution of the

101

problems of *imperium* and *libertas*. He depicted the Commonwealth as 'the "nature" of the British Empire defined, in Aristotelian fashion, by its end'.[5] Mansergh, in similar vein, in 1954, widened the scope and said: 'If the nature of the Commonwealth may be described teleologically its end is conceived to be the widening of a circle of self-governing peoples of differing cultural and racial origins within a community or a brotherhood of equal nations, linked by history ... '[6] Towards the end of the decolonization process, in 1969, he saw the outcome as a response to nationalist demands other than by counter-resistance or abdication – by, in fact, 'association, ultimately to be interpreted in terms of equality'.[7]

Yet, during the years of rapid rundown in the 1960s and 1970s, a tendency developed of downplaying the Commonwealth. Bruce Miller saw it in 1965 as 'a concert of convenience in which the prime consideration for each [state] is its own interest'. By 1973, he was putting it even more modestly: 'To provide something to belong to, to deal with unfinished colonial business ... and to serve as a link with history ... gave the Commonwealth a meaning.'[8] In 1982, Dennis Austin could see the Commonwealth 'moving away from ... any positive influence'.[9] And by 1992, Cain and Hopkins wrote simply, 'the empire sank, leaving only the ripples of the Commonwealth behind'.[10] As against this tendency to dismissal, Low argued that to view end-of-Empire simply as a concomitant of the decline of Britain as a great power 'only smacks of nostalgic myopia' and it neglects 'the profound sense of positive achievement ... ' To talk of the Commonwealth as 'altogether down and out is to be, quite simply, myopic'. It has, wrote Low, 'no real counterpart'.[11]

The process and the end-product must now be considered.

10

TRANSFERS OF POWER

For all the colourful drama of decolonization, the sheer size and span and speed of the half-a-lifetime transformation, and the infinite variety of the individual country experiences, the British approach displayed certain general characteristics. It was done by negotiation, did not precipitate great debate or political upheaval at home, and it was inextricably connected with the evolution of the Commonwealth.

First, in nearly all cases, decolonization was arranged by orderly transfers of power to democratically elected regimes. It did not stem from violent revolutions, military defeat (except, in part, for Burma) or by acts of retreat (except in Palestine, Aden, and perhaps, Somaliland and Vanuatu). Zimbabwe's UDI and its indecisive guerrilla war was exceptional, though these evoked memories of Ireland. And there were the 'Emergencies', with the use of force, in India, Malaya, the Gold Coast, Cyprus, Kenya, Nyasaland and British Guiana, but the negotiations were not conducted at the barrel of a gun. It is true that the processes of transfer, which had taken a reluctant half-century for India, became over-hasty by the 1960s, as the British sought successor-regimes with whom they hoped to co-operate. But, as Robert Menzies of Australia said in 1963, 'it was better to give independence a little too early in an atmosphere of friendship, than a little too late in an atmosphere of bitterness'. And Macleod, recalling his momentous two years at the Colonial Office wrote: 'Of course there were risks in moving quickly. But the risks of moving slowly were far greater.'[1]

The theme of orderly transfer to a co-operative regime had a long history. It was a continuation of a well-tried technique from the heyday of Empire. Indeed, Ronald Robinson, searching for a theory of imperialism which was also consistent with decolonization, developed a concept which had previously been used in relation to the Dominions.

Robinson and Gallagher had argued that responsible government in the Canadian and Australasian colonies had relieved Whitehall of the burdens of control, but maintained a community of interest between mother country and colonies, and that the British later moved to extend 'this technique of collaborating classes' to South Africa.[2]

In applying the 'collaborators' theory more generally, Robinson asked how a tiny handful of European pro-consuls could manipulate the complex societies of Asia and Africa and, later, how small nationalist élites could persuade the colonial rulers to go. His answer was that 'imperialism was as much a function of its victims' collaboration or non-collaboration' and to prepare for the endgame, 'Nationalists had to contrive a situation in which their rulers ran out of collaborators.' He called this the 'excentric' approach. If there were two circles – representing, on the one side, European economic drives and strategic imperatives and, on the other, the 'implacable continuities' of Asian and African societies – imperialism was not a true function of either but was 'excentric' to both.[3] He applied the same approach to decolonization. If organizing the permutations of collaboration 'constituted the true genius of colonial administration', from the 1940s the 'model went into reverse'.[4] Britain abandoned its traditional collaborators (e.g. Indian princes, Malay sultans, African kings and chiefs) and tried to create new democratic ones by the ballot-box. In doing this, they helped to manufacture the nationalist movements which led to the end of colonial rule. After transferring power to such collaborating regimes, they hoped that great power help with capital and military support would cement continuing co-operation. Hence, the concept of the 'Imperialism of Decolonization' whereby Cold War imperatives led the once anti-imperialist US to provide capital aid and military assistance to win over African nationalists from Marxian or pan-African and pan-Islamic influences. 'The formal Empire contracted ... as it had once expanded, as a variable function of integrating countries into the international capitalist economy', say Louis and Robinson, '... Visible empires may be abolished; the thraldom of international economy remains.'[5]

In all cases (except Palestine and Aden), Britain insisted on general elections by universal suffrage (usually several elections), to produce ruling groups to whom the reins of power could be transferred in an orderly manner. Often the last British governor stayed a while as the first Governor-General, British officers stayed on to train the local armed forces, British civil servants sometimes volunteered to continue in advisory roles, and various trade and defence agreements were made as further marks of continuity. In the case of Malaya and Singapore, the

Far East Strategic Reserve included units from Australia and New Zealand which stayed on even after the British withdrew in the 1970s. Much of this collaboration ended with the onset of military coups or the retirement of the British volunteers, but virtually all ex-colonies continued to collaborate in various regional and Commonwealth organizations.

The second major characteristic of the decolonization process was that it did not prompt a great debate about end-of-Empire in British politics. As we have seen, there was remarkably little inter-party fighting about decolonization. In so far as there was a great debate in post-war British politics, it was about Britain's relationship with Europe – with the EEC/EC/EU. The 'great debate about Empire' had already taken place over the future of India in the late 1920s and early 1930s, in the Simon Commission and the Round Table Conferences, in the Joint Select Committee on the Government of India Bill and the long debates in Parliament over the 1935 India Act. Low suggested that never again would the British political élite want to go through the same argument.[6] After the war, promises having been made to the Indians, it was a matter of finding the men and the moment for the demission of power. There was no similar protracted debate over independence for the Sudan, the Gold Coast or Malaya in the 1950s, only worries about the impact on the Commonwealth. There was nothing about the 'Wind of Change' in the Conservative manifesto in 1959. There were some last-minute delaying tactics in Central Africa from 'kith and kin Conservatives', but little debate about the withdrawal from East-of-Suez.

British politics did not experience the sort of political and constitutional upheavals which in France were occasioned by defeat at Dien Bien Phu and debate over the future of Algeria. True, there was a riot in Whitehall during the Suez crisis, but the Government was not toppled. American pressure ensured that Anthony Eden was dumped as prime minister (but it could be explained as ill-health), and Macmillan took over in a surprisingly smooth succession. There was shock and indignation in 1959 over the Hola killings in Kenya and the 'police state' in Nyasaland, but these were followed by an increased Conservative majority in the 'never had it so good' election of October 1959. There was nothing like the Portuguese coup of 1974, the vital prelude to decolonization in the Portuguese colonial empire. Above all, the dissolution of the British Empire bore no comparison with the sudden dissolution of the Soviet empire. Indeed, the momentous events of

1989–91 have almost consigned the British landmark years – 1947–8, 1959–61, 1967–8 – to the historical shadows. British politicians agonized about Northern Ireland and Europe, but they forgot about the Empire, and have been mainly indifferent to the Commonwealth.

Yet, the third characteristic which marks British decolonization is that it was very much connected with the Commonwealth. For, as the colonial rulers prepared to depart, they had well-known charts to follow, which marked out the well-trod stepping stones of constitutional evolution. From Crown colony or protectorate to representative government and responsible government, to Dominion status and on to full sovereignty and Commonwealth membership, was the route along which virtually all parts of the Empire passed. Dennis Austin has also stressed the significance of this process. Use of the ballot-box, increases in the representative seats in the legislative council, the promotion of un-officials on to the executive council had all been pioneered in the Dominions, elaborated with great ingenuity in the Indian Provinces, and put forward as a system for Africa by Andrew Cohen. Responsible government was the central technique. The executive was to be made responsible to the legislature; the Crown would act on the advice of ministers; there would be government by leaders of the parliamentary majority.

The passage could be effected in four different ways. The Governor could select his ministers. Then there was the full leap to a responsible Cabinet, as in the Canadian and Australasian colonies. There was the half leap to dyarchy, tried briefly in New Zealand and Jamaica in the nineteenth century, made explicitly in India, Burma and Malta in the 1920s and implicitly in Ceylon, the Gold Coast and elsewhere. Finally, Cohen's flexible, incremental method, whereby the proportion of unofficials in the legislative and executive councils could be adjusted gradually, was adopted in the West Indies, Africa and elsewhere from the 1940s and 1950s. By the age of acceleration after 1959, the experi-ence of such evolution was so ingrained that Austin suggests, 'Practice began to shape decisions by precedent and was thus brought into consciousness as policy.'[7] Alternative ideas, such as combining executive and legislative functions in a single body as in Donoughmore's State Council in Ceylon, 1931–46, were not effective, though they were revived in the Smaller Territories Enquiry Report of 1951, and tried briefly in the form of Governing Councils in the Solomons and the Gilbert and Ellice Islands in the 1970s. In no case did it prove satisfactory, so separate executive and legislative councils had to be restored, and the journey through to responsible government and the equivalent of Dominion status resumed.

Perhaps the most puzzling aspect of the process was the strange demise of Dominion status just at what seemed its moment of great triumph – the arrival of the three new Asian Dominions to attend the 1948 Prime Ministers' Meetings in Downing Street. Dominion status had long been accepted as the goal for India and, during the 1939–45 war, very specific promises of Dominion status after the war were made in respect of India, Burma and Ceylon. It was always stressed, from 1931, that Dominion status meant full independence and this could be either inside or outside the Commonwealth. And there was the precedent set by Eire, which had adopted a republican constitution, eliminated the Crown from its domestic arrangements, but remained externally associated with the Commonwealth and was still treated as a Dominion. Moreover, as negotiations proceeded in 1946 for finding ways of reaching the end of India's and Burma's road to independence, the interim governments of both countries were treated as if they were Dominions.

Yet, even in the 'old Dominions', Dominion status was increasingly felt to be a source of ambiguity. The style 'Dominions beyond the Seas' in the Royal Title, was deprecated in Canada – the pioneer Dominion. New Zealand joined the UN as 'New Zealand' and in January 1946 government departments in Wellington were told confidentially that, as 'Dominion of New Zealand' was obsolete and confusing as a description, they should use 'New Zealand' in official documents and letterheads, but do so without incurring publicity. There was misgiving about the constitutional meaning of Dominion status in South Africa. Although the idea of creating Dominions in India and Pakistan, before they drafted their independence constitutions, was adopted as a useful device to ensure a quick transfer of power in 1947 and facilitate their staying in the Commonwealth, when Burma tried to pull the same trick, it was firmly refused by the British Government. Ceylon became a Dominion at independence, but use of Dominion status was avoided by the Colonial Office in the preliminary constitutional instruments.

Once independence had been achieved in South Asia, resulting in three new Dominions and one seceding republic, discussion turned to how the Commonwealth could accommodate the republic India was determined to become. Informal discussions were held about this during the 1948 Prime Ministers' Meetings, before which Attlee sent Brook, the Cabinet Secretary, to Ottawa, Canberra and Wellington to sound the premiers' opinions. As a result, it was suggested that 'Dominion' should be dropped as a description in favour of 'Commonwealth Country' or 'Member of the Commonwealth', and that 'Dominion status' should be superseded by the formulation 'fully independent members of the Commonwealth' and that 'British' should be omitted in front of 'Commonwealth of Nations'.[8] None of these changes were adopted formally, but at the end of 1948, Cabinet ministers and senior officials were circularized by Attlee about these matters of 'nomenclature'.[9] Old habits died hard. In 1949, Brook admitted that even in the Cabinet Office he had trouble with 'chaps who use "old Dominions" and "new Dominions"' and he could not think of suitable alternatives. In the CRO they did some 'head-scratching' without much effect: 'Somebody here suggested "original", but you only have to put the letters "ab" before it to see the sort of pitfalls in this!'[10]

Nevertheless, in the mid-1950s, Dominion status faded away after being demanded by the Gold Coast and Singapore. The Gold Coast became the test case. As soon as he won the 1951 election, Nkrumah called for Dominion status in the Commonwealth at the earliest moment. This immediately excited adverse comment in South Africa and a realization in the CRO that the implications of an African Dominion needed study because of likely repercussions elsewhere. A joint CRO/Colonial Office working party reported that the Gold Coast demand raised the question about 'the terminus of constitutional change' for other colonies and whether self-government in the Commonwealth – the official policy – meant 'Membership of the Commonwealth' as then understood.[11] The Secretary of State for Colonies defused the immediate issue by making it clear that while the granting of self-government was a British Government responsibility, Dominion status and Commonwealth membership were for decision by the other members collectively. In the Colonial Office they were keen that these processes should be 'synchronized' so self-governing countries simply stayed as Commonwealth members – 'if we do in fact want more Ceylons and fewer Burmas'.[12]

Concern for the niceties of nomenclature led to Cabinet agreement, on 1 December 1955, that 'full self-government' should be used instead of 'independence' on the ground that the latter usage might imply the probability of secession from the Commonwealth. Along with this went the suggestion that 'full membership of the Commonwealth' was preferred to 'independence within the Commonwealth'.[13] When a Canadian official tried a definition of membership in 1960, he came up simply with: 'those independent, sovereign nations who have been accepted as full members for the purpose of the Prime Ministers'

Meetings'.[14] The British Cabinet Secretary noted that membership had been confined to 'significant countries which could expect to exercise some influence in world counsels, to be viable economically, and to be worthwhile partners in some regional defence system'.[15] Dominion status dropped out of the debate, except for a belated revival by the Fijians, but Commonwealth membership was the subject of endless agonizing and dramatic change.

11

REPUBLICS IN THE COMMONWEALTH

If Commonwealth doctrines and procedures shaped the processes of decolonization in India, Burma and Ceylon, decolonization and its aftermath completely reshaped the Commonwealth. In this respect, India's continued membership as a republic became the most significant landmark in the evolution of the modern Commonwealth, by providing a new dimension to the doctrine of equality of status enunciated in 1926 and 1931.[1]

Even before partition had been agreed upon, there was a realization that Commonwealth relations would have to be adapted. On 8 November 1946, Sir David Monteath, the Permanent Under-Secretary of the India Office, approached his opposite numbers in Whitehall for their views on Indian membership and what changes in Commonwealth relations would be necessary to cater for India, Burma and other Asian countries. For the Dominions Office, Sir Eric Machtig said it was desirable to keep India in; if it went out the Commonwealth would be weakened. From the Foreign Office, Sir Orme Sargent gave the same view and said that India's departure would be a blow to British prestige. The Chiefs of Staff also regarded India as strategically important. But from the Colonial Office, Sir George Gater doubted whether India's membership would be a good model for the colonial Empire; a reluctant member could be a liability.[2]

A new dimension to this debate was added, in December 1946, by Nehru's announcement of the goal of a sovereign independent republic. As the Indian Office collated the replies of the other departments, it now asked whether the new-style Commonwealth relations could include a republic. During an officials' meeting in the India Office on 11 March 1947, three options for India were mooted: full Commonwealth membership including allegiance to the Crown; a republic on the Eire external association model; or a foreign state with close treaty relations. It was agreed that Eire was not a good precedent, and the Colonial Office representative deprecated any 'hybrid status' as a bad example for the rest of the Empire.[3]

Keeping India in the Commonwealth was declared by Mountbatten as his 'single most important problem'. By mid-1947, on the eve of partition, the quest for a looser form of Commonwealth was exercising minds in many quarters. Dominion status was being eagerly grasped as the procedural device to speed the transfer of power in India. And from New Zealand, Peter Fraser nodded approval by venturing his much-to-be-quoted aphorism that Dominion status was 'independence with something added, and not independence with something taken away'.[4] But Brook, the Cabinet Secretary, was warning Attlee that they needed to find a better form of association as India was not the only problem. They had to consider the position of Eire, South Africa, Burma and Ceylon. He passed on an idea from Sir Walter Monckton, a prominent lawyer acting as constitutional adviser to the Nizam of Hyderabad, who suggested they needed a solution which did not retain the King as 'Head of state of India'. Monckton thought there was the 'germ of an idea' in the concept of common citizenship with allegiance to the King as 'Head of the association'.[5]

Attlee was receptive to these calls for a flexible approach. In a circular to ministers on 19 May 1947, he said they had to find a formula which would enable the greatest number of countries to adhere to the Commonwealth without excessive uniformity in their internal constitutions. On 9 June 1947, he set up a new ministerial committee on Commonwealth relations. On the very same day, support for the idea of association without allegiance to the Crown came from Governor Rance of Burma. Although he had just firmly told the Burmese leaders that if they wanted a republic it would be outside the Commonwealth, when he wrote to Lord Listowel (the Secretary of State for Burma), Mountbatten (the Viceroy), Lord Killearn (the Commissioner-General in Southeast Asia) and Malcolm Macdonald (the Governor-General), Rance expressed anxiety over the effect Burma's departure would have on Ceylon and Malaya and said he would prefer the Commonwealth as a voluntary association.

Malcolm Macdonald's response endorsed Rance's anxiety about possible defections. If Burma and India left the Commonwealth, he predicted an immense decline in 'our prestige and position in Southeast Asia'. He believed they stood at 'one of the great testing moments of British statesmanship'. How could the 'colonial part' of the Empire be transformed into free and equal nations? He resurrected the Eire model, which he had supported as Secretary of State for Dominions Affairs in 1937, because he thought then that India and Burma might want to follow Eire's example. He wondered if the Irish model could be adapted for a Burmese republic recognizing the King as 'head of the Commonwealth' and supreme authority in matters of external affairs.[6] Macdonald's suggestion was considered seriously by the Cabinet's India and Burma Committee, but it felt that the Eire model was inappropriate in view of India's acceptance of Dominion status.

As the debate proceeded in 1948, and an official committee studied the future of the Commonwealth in preparation for Attlee's ministerial committee, two further dimensions were added. First, the possibility of a two-tier Commonwealth was raised in a memo from R. J. Stent, an ex-Indian civil servant now working for the Foreign Office, who suggested that Asian countries would not accept a white king. He mooted the idea of associate membership, suggesting that consideration be given to a 'Commonwealth of British and Associated States'. Secondly, it tran-spired that the Eire model was about to be lost. In February 1948, de Valera's government went out of office and the British Representative in Dublin, Lord Rugby, reported that the new ministry of John A. Costello might repeal the External Relations Act. Thus, as Attlee's Government sought a design for the New Commonwealth, the emerging questions were: would the Republic of Ireland depart?; could India stay as a republic?

Attlee made a preliminary approach to Nehru on 11 March 1948, pointing out that the Commonwealth was not based on theory but on the application of democratic principles. He said that in actuality countries like Australia and New Zealand had more real freedom than most South American republics. The only link in the Commonwealth was through the Crown – was there any objection to India maintaining common allegiance to the Crown? Attlee even wondered whether 'state' rather than 'republic' could be used in the Indian constitution.[7]

To the ministerial committee, when it met on 12 April 1948, Attlee said the Indian republic issue raised the whole question of Common-wealth membership in 'an acute form'. He put to his colleagues three options: they could 'dilute' the constitutional relationship to include a republic; they could confine membership to those who accepted existing arrangements; or they could go to a two-tier system. By the next meeting on 31 May 1948, the officials' committee were recommending that the bonds of Commonwealth were 'intangible and undefinable'. They did not think new members should be confronted with formal principles, and they recommended nomenclature changes like dropping 'Dominion'. Their main suggestion was that the Crown might be recognized as 'Supreme Head of the Commonwealth', with a formal role only in external affairs. This could become the basic mark of membership and the Royal Title might include the rubric 'Head of all countries of the Commonwealth of Nations'.[8]

Before the Prime Ministers' Meetings convened in October 1948, Attlee sent Brook to talk with the Canadian, Australian and New Zealand prime ministers. He found them all uneasy about the three Asian Dominions with whom they felt no shared heritage and sentiment, but they recognized that the Commonwealth's influence would decline if India followed Burma and left. No effort should be spared to keep India's membership, and tolerance of a few constitutional anomalies was seen as a small price to pay provided that the existing relationships of the 'central members' – Britain, Canada, Australia and New Zealand – were not disturbed. They all preferred that India should accept the Crown for some purposes. By the time the prime ministers got together in London in October 1948, the Irish prime minister, on a visit to Ottawa, had dropped the bombshell that, not only would Eire repeal the External Relations Act, but it would leave the Commonwealth.[9] So the 'external association' card had been removed from the pack.

There were informal discussions during the Prime Ministers' Meetings, but apart from the suggested nomenclature changes, nothing was decided about India. Nehru was made aware that the role of the Crown was seen as crucial, but when he subsequently stated his terms in a memorandum of 11 December 1948, his concessions were slight: India must be recognized as a republic; he would accept a common citizenship and treat Commonwealth countries as not 'foreign' in treaties and legislation; where India had no ambassador it would use Common-wealth representatives, and the President of India would act on behalf of the Crown in fulfilling obligations to non-Indian Commonwealth citizens within India. Attlee replied to Nehru on 16 December 1948 that this was not satisfactory for membership through the nexus of the Crown.

The problem was discussed with Krishna Menon, the Indian High Commissioner, at a meeting on 22 December 1948, by Attlee, Cripps and Patrick Gordon-Walker, the Parliamentary Under-Secretary for Commonwealth Relations whom Attlee entrusted with the preparatory work on the matter. Cripps and Attlee agreed, initially, that a link through the Crown was essential and that without it there would be a different sort of relationship. Menon said this would imply a two-tier system which India opposed. It did not want to emulate Eire; India would be 'in or out'. Attlee felt there was no way round some link through the Crown, but Cripps thought it should not be impossible to devise 'some nexus between the Crown and a Republic'.[10] After this discussion, Gordon-Walker wrote a paper on 'The Link with India' which would provide the vital conceptual breakthrough in the resolution of the republican issue.

Gordon-Walker began by considering what minimum conditions would be asked of India by the other members. Some role for the Crown should be sought, such as in the appointment of the president of India, or in the appointment of ambassadors, or in a statement that the president acted on powers delegated by the Crown. If there was any chance of devising a satisfactory Crown link, he felt they should try. He then introduced a completely different approach. Could they not base the relationship on 'the will and intent' of all the members? They could frankly face the problem of fitting a republic into the Commonwealth alongside what he called the 'Crown Dominions':

> What I have in mind is not a weakening of the connection through the Crown to the lowest permissible point but the deliberate and friendly snapping of the Crown-link by mutual consent and the simultaneous absorption of a completely non-monarchical Dominion into the Commonwealth, but a Dominion that genuinely and sincerely wishes to remain in the Commonwealth.[11]

He suggested simultaneous declarations by India and the other members indicating that India was in the Commonwealth and would be treated as such by the rest.

Gordon-Walker suggested that 'various embellishments' might be retained and the King might well become Head of a Commonwealth that consisted in part of 'Crown Dominions' (of which he would also be King) and in part of a Republican Dominion or Dominions. He said it would be a tragedy if, given India's goodwill, they failed to achieve agreement. The ministerial committee took the matter up again on 7 January 1949, when Attlee put forward three options: India could enter some special form of 'association'; it could be treated as a foreign state in close treaty relations; or the structure of the Commonwealth could be altered to permit the membership of a republic. All the other member governments, said Attlee, were unanimous in wanting a solution, and he also emphasized that the colonial Empire would be 'gravely affected by failure of the Commonwealth to adjust itself'.[12] A number of ministerial misgivings were voiced, so the matter went back to the officials.

Brook admitted to the official committee on 11 January 1949 that he doubted Nehru would accept the Crown link. They had to consider the admission of a republic to full membership. Their starting point, he suggested, should be criteria for membership derived from the 1926 Balfour Report. In this context, members were (i) sovereign states, (ii) equal in status, (iii) not foreign in relation to each other, (iv) communities which owe, or formerly owed, allegiance to the Crown, (v) were freely associated, (vi) were united in accepting certain principles and practices of consultation, and (vii) were united by common citizenship. In a subsequent meeting, on 4 February 1949, the officials tried to recast the 1926 definition in a form which dispensed with common allegiance. From this, a formula seemed possible which would include an affirm-ation of the sovereignty of members; the concept of equal partnership; the practice of not treating members as foreign; and a statement of India's continued membership under a republican constitution. Such a declaration would stem from a 'common act of will' and the main argument for it would be 'historical continuity'.[13]

This proposal came before the ministerial committee on 8 February 1949, when Lord Chancellor Jowitt raised issues about international recognition and most-favoured-nation treaties, but these were regarded as secondary. It was agreed that the cardinal point was India's desire to remain a member. Ministers realized that to insist on terms which made this impossible would not only be a 'grave failure of statesmanship', it might have a 'corroding and disintegrating effect' on the rest of the Commonwealth.[14] It was proposed they should call a full Common-wealth conference in April, after preliminary consultations with member governments. This was agreed by the Cabinet on 9 February 1949, though Bevin remained sceptical about the value of India's membership.

Attlee now sent personal emissaries to all the member capitals. Brook went to Ottawa. Gordon-Walker went to Karachi, Colombo and then to New Delhi. He was told to stress the need for the Crown link and also to play the Cold War card, that retaining India's membership would help uphold Commonwealth influence in combating communism in Southeast Asia. Lord Listowel was the messenger to Wellington and Canberra, and Sir Percivale Liesching talked with the South African prime minister and with Smuts. The most serious misgivings were encountered in New Zealand. Fraser was concerned about unity in wartime. He feared a 'flabby Commonwealth' and said, 'The British Empire is not founded on negations.'[15]

On the eve of the special conference in April 1949 Gordon-Walker was pessimistic. He did not think their 'chances at all good'. But he hoped they could avoid an impasse and felt agreement to delay a decision might be the most likely outcome.[16] Attlee was more sanguine. He suggested that they should try first for the Crown link and common allegiance; if this failed, they should seek a different sort of link. He felt that the most helpful concept would be recognition of the King as 'Head of the Commonwealth' – the idea which had been variously proposed by de Valera back in 1922 and, more recently, by Walter Monckton, Malcolm Macdonald, Gordon-Walker and the senior officials' committee. Alternative draft declarations were prepared – a single one which all could adhere to, or separate ones by India and the rest. Both formulations included recognition of King George VI as 'Head of the Commonwealth and the symbol of the free association' of the independent members.[17]

Four days before the meetings started in Downing Street, Eire left the Commonwealth. There had been plenty of warning. Indeed, when Costello had moved the Republic of Ireland Bill in the *Dáil* on 24 November 1948, he said it would 'end forever, in a simple, clear and unequivocal way this country's long and tragic association with the institutions of the British Crown'.[18] It was ironical, therefore, that at the opening meeting of the Prime Ministers' Meetings on 22 April 1949, Nehru said India wished to remain a member and would accept the King as symbol of the free association. The Canadian, Australian and New Zealand representatives could not accept anything which impaired their countries' loyalty to the Crown. It was Daniel Malan of South Africa (the new boy of the conference) who said it was time to relax common allegiance as the Commonwealth derived from 'factors less tangible but even more potent'.[19] After these preliminaries, it was agreed that a possible declaration would be presented after the weekend.

Later on the first day, however, Attlee, Cripps and Brook had a private meeting with Nehru when the latter expressed his misgivings about 'Head of the Commonwealth'. His Cabinet had only approved accepting the King as 'symbol of free association'. 'Head' might imply 'some kind of super-state'. But Cripps argued that the King would be Head because he was a symbol: 'It was this symbolism, and nothing more, that created the "Headship".' Nehru said he might persuade his colleagues to accept 'Head' *as* symbol instead of *and* symbol.[20] At a private meeting among the other representatives, the Pakistan and Ceylon prime ministers expressed doubts as to whether India would fulfil the obligations of membership. Pakistan professed to be worried about the Soviet threat. And both realized that the republican precedent was one they, too, might have to follow. When he reported progress to the British Cabinet in the evening, Attlee encountered insistence by Bevin that the outcome should not weaken Britain's influence in Southeast Asia and the Far East.

As the conference reconvened after the weekend to consider the draft declaration, it was Malan, again, who was most concerned about the concept of 'Head of the Commonwealth', which could appear to represent a fundamental change in the structure of the Commonwealth. But Nehru now said he could accept 'Head of the Commonwealth' if it would help the other members to find an agreed solution. This was reached on 26 April, after Malan had again voiced anxieties that 'Headship' might imply some constitutional role in the Commonwealth as a whole. He was only mollified by the formula recognizing the King as the symbol of the free association of the independent member nations and '*as such* Head of the Commonwealth' and agreement to a confidential minute confirming that the King had no constitutional role within South Africa. In another confidential minute (on Liquat Ali Khan of Pakistan's insistence) it was accepted that further requests for republican status would be entertained by subsequent meetings and could expect similar approval.

On 27 April, the conference gathered informally at Buckingham Palace and offered George VI, the last Emperor of India, the results of their labours. The London Declaration, which built on the Balfour Report of 1926, would become the foundation document of the 'New Commonwealth'. The opening paragraph, using the old style, listed the governments of the 'British Commonwealth of Nations' which owed common allegiance to the Crown and stated their consideration of India's impending constitutional changes. It went on:

> The Government of India have informed the other Governments of the Commonwealth of the intention of the Indian people that under the new constitution which is about to be adopted India shall become a sovereign independent Republic. The Government of India have, however, declared and affirmed India's desire to continue her full membership of the Commonwealth of Nations and her acceptance of The King as the symbol of the free association of its independent member nations and as such the Head of the Commonwealth.
>
> The Governments of the other countries of the Commonwealth the basis of whose membership of the Commonwealth is not hereby changed, accept and recognise India's continuing membership in accordance with the terms of this declaration.

The final paragraph declared, in the new style, that the free and equal members remained united in the 'Commonwealth of Nations, freely co-operating in the pursuit of peace, liberty and progress'.[21] After more than two years of intense discussion, India thus set the precedent which the majority of new members would eventually follow. The poignant paradox was that only eight days separated the Republic of Ireland's departure and India's acceptance as a republic.

But the conference had not quite ended. During a final meeting on 27 April 1949, it was agreed that the Royal Title would be 'locally variable' through separate legislation in member parliaments. And the conference closed on an entirely different note, occasioned by Peter Fraser's call for solidarity in wartime. 'Could they be confident in the future, as they had been confident in the past, that Commonwealth countries would all stand together in an emergency in support of a just cause?' Liaquat Ali Khan asked the same question. But Nehru de-precated the emphasis on military defence. Asia was in turmoil because of low living conditions and such conditions encouraged the spread of communism. Fraser doubted whether it was possible to avoid division of the world into power blocs, but Nehru, while agreeing that countries had to prepare to defend themselves, said it was more important to prevent the political encroachments of communism.[22] It is usually overlooked that this landmark conference, which heralded the modern Commonwealth and settled the crucial issue of republican membership, ended up discussing the Cold War, that all-pervasive background element to the age of decolonization.

12

THE COMMONWEALTH: DISILLUSIONMENT, DETACHMENT AND REDISCOVERY

As decolonization accelerated, the Commonwealth was forced to catch up. During the race, however, British reluctance raised caution signs all along the way. As ever, virtue was always made of necessity, and change was presented publicly with a positive ring. But there was growing disillusionment in Britain about the Commonwealth just at the very moment when the association was evolving into a multilateral international organization with a momentum of its own.

Each major watershed of decolonization made its mark on the Commonwealth by establishing vital precedents. The republic debate in 1947–9 involved the loss of Burma and Ireland, but the decision over India set the precedent for many other republics, which would soon constitute the majority of its members. The debate in the 1950s over a mezzanine status or a two-tier Commonwealth, sparked off by the Gold Coast demand for Dominion status, induced a realization that, if independent Ghana was denied full membership, there would be little chance of keeping the rest of Africa in the Commonwealth. The debate over Cyprus membership in 1960–1, and the recognition that 'all the rest of the tiddlers' would follow its example, paved the way for the small mini and micro states, which would eventually account for over half of the membership. The three precedents meant that by the time of the 'Wind of Change', Commonwealth membership had become a badge automatically available to newly independent states.

These developments, which were welcomed with considerable optimistic rhetoric by enthusiasts like the 'Expanding Commonwealth

Group' of MPs, did not please certain elements of the British political establishment. Looking back on the Indian decision from 1953, Lord Swinton, Churchill's Commonwealth Secretary, said, 'I doubt we shall ever escape the unhappy results of that fatal decision.' And his arch-Conservative colleague, Lord Salisbury (a former Commonwealth Secretary), felt the presence of the Asian Dominions had completely destroyed the atmosphere which had previously existed in the Commonwealth.[1]

Although the two-tier concept was firmly rejected each time it came up, a *de facto* two-tier system operated in preliminary informal consultations the British had with Canada, Australia and New Zealand before major Commonwealth meetings. After the Suez crisis, Prime Minister Sidney Holland of New Zealand so feared that the old members would be 'drowned' by the new that he advocated an advisory council of the former, to hold the 'hard core' together.[2] Macmillan was bitterly disappointed when, at the same 1961 Prime Ministers' Meetings, as he welcomed Cyprus for the first time, South Africa chose to quit the Commonwealth because members insisted on discussing the policy of apartheid in connection with the Union's application to become a republic. A year later, Macmillan confessed privately to Menzies that 'I now shrink from any Commonwealth meeting because I know how troublesome it will be'.[3] Early in 1962, Sir Norman Brook warned Macmillan that there would be 'another rush of candidates for full membership', as advances to independence were coming more rapidly than 'anything we had envisaged'.[4] The total membership might soon reach eighteen and, by 1970, it could be between twenty-one and thirty-five. The low point in attitudes about the Commonwealth was reached in the second half of the 1960s. In 1965, a feature writer on *The Times* (reportedly Enoch Powell), dubbed the Commonwealth 'a gigantic farce', and Rhodesia's UDI was followed by calls that Britain be kicked out of the Commonwealth. Military coups followed in quick succession in Nigeria, Ghana and Sierra Leone, while Britain was preoccupied with economic crises, the withdrawal from East-of-Suez, and renewed attempts to join the EEC.

By now, however, the Commonwealth had become detached from Whitehall and had embarked on a new life focusing on the quieter surroundings of Pall Mall, where the Secretariat was establishing itself in the elegant Royal Palace of Marlborough House. Yet this development had come as something of a surprise.

In the preparations for the 1964 Prime Ministers' Meetings, the British, making their usual preliminary approaches to the Canadian,

Australian and New Zealand Governments, noted a 'crisis of confidence' in the Commonwealth and proposed some practical ways of catching the imagination of the new members. A programme entitled 'The Way Ahead' involved schemes for technical assistance, development projects, capital aid for higher education, training and research in public administration, and the creation of a foundation with funds to foster professional and unofficial links. In the discussions about these ideas, the old members were considerably surprised when Nkrumah (now a veteran of these gatherings) called for a 'central clearing house' for aid, trade, and development plans and for the circulation of information. Obote specifically proposed a central secretariat. They were supported by Eric Williams of Trinidad, who also proposed a Commonwealth fund for development.

The British proposals were, in fact, overtaken by the secretariat concept – something that had always been resisted in the days of Dominion status. A secretariat as a 'visible symbol of the spirit of co-operation' was envisaged. Senior officials examined the idea and drafted an agreed memorandum depicting a secretariat designed to facilitate consultation but not to arrogate to itself executive functions. This was approved in 1965. The Foundation, as a separate autonomous body, housed within the Secretariat, came into being in the following year, to administer a voluntary fund to improve links between Commonwealth organizations in professional fields.[5]

From the mid-1960s, as Whitehall closed the files on distant islands, withdrew from East-of-Suez, and endured opprobrium for not healing the UDI canker or for failing to take a tough enough line with South Africa over apartheid, the organizing of Commonwealth consultations and conferences at the official, ministerial or heads of government level was taken over by the Secretariat. As membership grew steadily, with the independence of more and more small, republican countries, the association took on an ethos very different from that intimate, unwritten alliance of Britain and the old Dominions which had comprised the old Commonwealth of Nations.

The Cabinet Secretary's alarmed prediction about the size of the Commonwealth, made in the aftermath of the Cyprus debate, was not far off the mark. If his fear of eighteen members by mid-1963 over-estimated an actual figure of fifteen at that date, this had doubled by the end of the decade. By the end of 1970, the total of thirty-one was at the upper end of Brook's twenty-one to thirty-five range. Four more years elapsed before it hit thirty-five, but by the end of 1980 it had reached forty-five. Ten years later, Namibia became the fiftieth member and

South Africa's return, in 1994, brought the total to the same as the initial UN membership in 1945. Cameroon joined in 1995 in time to attend the Auckland CHOGM, which announced the acceptance of Mozambique – the first non-ex-British colony – bringing the total to fifty-three, although Nigeria was under suspension.[6] Fiji returned in 1997 to make the total fifty-four. Twenty-eight out of this total – more than half – had populations of less than a million at independence, thus confirming the tiddlers tendency.

The evolution of this new Commonwealth may be summarized by a brief survey of five trends which emerged during the first thirty years of the Secretariat. They were the years when the Commonwealth was (i) de-Britannicized, (ii) regionalized, (iii) globalized, and, more recently, (iv) recomposed and, increasingly, (v) privatized.

The first Secretary-General, Arnold Smith from Canada, stressed from the start that he was the servant of the Heads of Government collectively, not an adjunct of Whitehall. He adopted as a virtual motto the adage 'consultation was the lifeblood of the Commonwealth' and its mission was 'enlarging the vision of the members'.[7] At the time of UDI, he persuaded the Tanzanian and Ghanaian Governments, which broke off relations with Britain, not to quit the Commonwealth since it was as much a Canadian creation as a British one. Under his prompting, the Commonwealth Fund for Technical Co-operation was created in 1971, as the operational arm of the Secretariat for providing experts for technical assistance in planning, training and market development.

The trend to de-Britannicization was accentuated by the approach of the second Secretary-General, Sonny Ramphal, a flamboyant Guyanan, who perfected a speaking style noted for alliterative antitheses. He once said that he assumed member governments wanted a secretariat 'that is effective without being expansive, that is dynamic without being diffusive, that can grow without being grandiose'. He called the Commonwealth a 'bridge and not a bloc', 'a fellowship not a forum', and said its business was 'conversion rather than confrontation'. In an address to the Royal Commonwealth Society in 1976, he said that the Commonwealth 'is not an evolution from empire sustained by memory and justified by sentiment. It is a negation of empire – a community of free and equal members sustained by the practicalities of cooperation and justified by the needs of our global society.'[8] By the 1980s, as the apartheid regime in South Africa became increasingly isolated and Commonwealth conferences increasingly preoccupied with anti-apartheid tactics, the British, under Mrs Thatcher's leadership, broke consensus on this issue, thus emphasizing the de-Britannicizing trend. From 1986 to 1989, Britain seemed increasingly detached from certain major Commonwealth concerns. Although interest revived in the 1990s, Baroness Chalker reminded the House of Commons Foreign Affairs Committee in 1995 that 'we are not, as the United Kingdom, the head country of the Commonwealth'.[9]

African preoccupations also illustrated the regionalizing trend, which was consistent with a growing tendency of states to enter enlarged groupings with their neighbours. It was a trend most forcibly advanced by the European Communities and this, in turn, prompted other regions to organize for trade access – as in the Lomé Conventions – to gain a stronger voice in negotiations. All member countries became involved in regional groupings. Australia and New Zealand had made the Canberra Pact in 1944, and by the 1980s had a Closer Economic Relations agreement looking towards a single market. Singapore, Malaysia and Brunei were in the Association of Southeast Asian Nations (ASEAN), founded in 1967. The South Pacific Forum, started in 1971, began as a Commonwealth grouping which expanded to fifteen members. In the Caribbean, CARICOM was formed in 1973 to negotiate with the EC, and the smaller islands also joined in the Organization of East Caribbean States with a goal of integration. African members, as well as joining the Organization of African Unity, became involved in the Economic Community of West African States (ECOWAS), formed in Lagos in 1975, or the Southern African Development Co-ordination Conference (1980), which, in 1992, became the Southern African Development Community (SADC). The Asian members joined with smaller neighbours to form the South Asian Association for Regional Co-operation in 1985 (SAARC). Britain's final entry into the EEC in 1973 had, of course, coincided with the closing phases of the 'Wind of Change', just before the final withdrawal from East-of-Suez.

A further example of the regionalizing trend could be seen in the evolution of the CHOGMs. Since 1969, they have only been held in Britain twice – in 1977 on the Silver Jubilee of the Queen's reign, and in 1997, the Golden Jubilee of the ending of the Raj. Starting in Singapore in 1971, the meetings, held biennially, went to Ottawa, Kingston, Lusaka, Melbourne, Delhi, Nassau, Vancouver, Kuala Lumpur, Harare, Limassol and Auckland. Opening speakers were always, until 1997, selected to provide regional balance. Spotting 'whose turn next' and the venue for future meetings became a journalistic art.

Yet, as Commonwealth members concentrated on their neighbour-hoods, they also became increasingly aware that their problems had much wider implications. Thus a globalizing trend became unavoidable. Arnold Smith was fond of saying that members 'need to learn to share the planet'. At Singapore in 1971, a Declaration was adopted by which members pledged themselves to adhere to 'certain principles in common'. In a statement, prepared by President Kaunda of Zambia, the members professed themselves *in favour* of peace, liberty and co-operation and *against* racial discrimination, colonial domination and wide inequalities of wealth.[10] Ramphal, who had been Vice-President of the UN General Assembly and, indeed, a one-time candidate for the UN Secretary-Generalship, was an eloquent exponent of Commonwealth contributions to global concerns. His most celebrated aphorism was: 'The Commonwealth cannot negotiate for the world, but it can help the world to negotiate.'[11] And he was a member of all four of the great independent international commissions on global issues in the 1980s – the Brandt Commission on development, the Palme Commission on disarmament and security, the Brundtland Commission on the environment, and the Nyerere Commission on South–South Co-operation – for whose endeavours the Secretariat gave back-up support. Under Ramphal's guidance a succession of Commonwealth expert groups (of 'Ten Wise Men') from different regions were assembled to make authoritative reports on global problems such as economic restructuring, development, protectionism, debt, climate changes, vulnerability and women's rights. It could be argued that there was much study, many excellent reports, a certain amount of rhetoric, and little action.

However, in the new atmosphere of the 1990s, with the collapse of the Soviet Empire and the welling up of ethno-nationalisms within many member states, there was a new emphasis on human rights. As Ramphal's fifteen years as Secretary-General gave way, in 1990, to the term of Chief Emeka Anyaoku from Nigeria, a high level appraisal group of ten heads of government and their advisers went to work to examine the role of the Commonwealth in the 1990s. At the 1991 CHOGM, held in Zimbabwe, the Harare Commonwealth Declaration reaffirmed the principles of 1971 and went on to pledge support for some more specific 'fundamental political values'. These included democracy, the rule of law, independent judiciaries, just and honest administration, fundamental human rights, gender equality and universal access to education.[12] In 1995, at the Auckland CHOGM, some measures for monitoring adherence to these principles were adopted and Nigeria's membership of the Commonwealth was suspended because of recent actions of that country's military rulers.

The annulment of a presidential election and incarceration of the supposed victor, and imprisonment of political dissidents, including a former head of state, had culminated in the execution, on the verdict of a special court, of nine regional and environmental activists at the very moment the heads of government were in conference. It came as a snub the CHOGM could not accept without losing credibility.

Such a decisive action as suspending a member country may be viewed against the recomposing trend which emerged in the mid-1980s. Advantage was taken of the new communications technology. This did not mean that the Commonwealth was becoming 'centralized' or was taking on the character of a super-state, but that it had found new modes of co-operative action.

As a response to the drastic decline in student mobility brought about by the full cost-recovery fee regime adopted by the more developed member countries, notably Britain, Ramphal suggested exploring the possibilities for distance learning. A panel chaired by Lord Briggs, head of an Oxford college and Chancellor of the Open University, recommended in 1987 a Commonwealth University for Co-operation in Distance Learning with the visionary goal of ensuring that 'any learner, anywhere in the Commonwealth shall be able to study any distance-teaching programme available from any bona fide college or university in the Commonwealth'.[13] In 1988, the Commonwealth of Learning, COL, was established in Vancouver BC, not as an institution to enrol students, but as a training and advisory body in distance-learning technique and a brokerage organization for sharing distance-learning programmes throughout the Commonwealth. COLIS (the COL Information Services Network) was created as a computer database listing available distance-learning courses.

Also online were a series of Commonwealth Liaison Units (CLUs) established in nearly forty member countries as networking co-ordinators among Non-Governmental Organizations (NGOs).[14] These CLUs, established in many cases with grants for their communications equipment from the Commonwealth Foundation, were designed to link up NGOs at the national, regional and Commonwealth-wide levels. Also in keeping with the trend towards online connections, COMNET, the Commonwealth Network for Information Technology was created in 1990, and a Commonwealth Business Network (COMBINET) was attempted in 1994, and the Secretariat created a Web Site in 1997.

This recomposing tendency, the applications for membership from Cameroon and Mozambique, the new atmosphere apparent at the end of the Cold War, and the dismantling of apartheid combined to prompt a rediscovery of the Commonwealth in Britain. At the Harare CHOGM, in 1991, the conciliatory stance of John Major, the prime minister, was in marked contrast to Mrs Thatcher's 'one against forty-eight' attitude.[15] The Harare Declaration was largely influenced by British officials behind the scenes. At the end of 1994, the Foreign Affairs Committee of the House of Commons embarked on an inquiry into the role of the Commonwealth. The task took them more than a year and involved, as well as hearings in Westminster, visits to Canada, Jamaica, Barbados, St Lucia, Kenya, Uganda, South Africa, India, Pakistan, Bangladesh, Malaysia, Australia and New Zealand. It reported somewhat defensively in 1996 that: 'Perhaps it was understandable for a few decades after the end of Empire that the Commonwealth was seen in the United Kingdom as a relic of an imperial past – a political albatross around the country's neck.' But the committee members had formed a much more positive view and concluded, 'that era is over, and so is its successor phase of "decolonisation"'. In the new global pattern the committee found the Commonwealth gave Britain 'both friends and opportunities'.[16]

Finally, the ethos of the 1990s was conducive to the 'privatization' of the Commonwealth. At the ideological level this found expression in the Harare Declaration in which democracy, the rule of law, just government and human rights were seen as concomitants of sustainable development, sound economic management, the 'central role of the market economy', and the 'freest possible flow of multilateral trade'.[17] As Stephen Chan put it – this was the ideology of the victors of the Cold War. At the practical level, it involved a growing partnership with private enterprise as in the Commonwealth Equity Fund, launched in Kuala Lumpur in 1989; the Commonwealth Partnership in Technology Management, started in 1995 as a non-profit company providing advisory and technical services for technological upgrading; and the Commonwealth Private Investment Initiative also launched in Auckland. Also privatized in 1996 was the production of *The Commonwealth Handbook* and in 1997 CHOGM accommodation bookings.

But the most significant aspect of the privatizing trend is the emphasis and recognition given to the NGOs in the Commonwealth. These had developed at three levels, which were increasingly encouraged and utilized by the official Commonwealth. First came the professional organizations. The earliest dated from the heyday of Empire – the Press Union (1909), the Parliamentary Association (1911), the Universities Association (1913) and the Forestry Association (1921). They were joined, after the 1939–45 war, by associations concerned with broadcasting, engineers, government science, the blind and the deaf. However, the real flowering came with the creation of the Foundation. Since the 1960s, some thirty new associations were created, with Foundation support.[18]

A second group of NGOs, which sometimes overlapped with the first, operated in the care and welfare fields for which a *Guidelines for Good Policy and Practice*, approved at an NGO Forum in Wellington in 1995, was dubbed the 'Geneva Convention' of the NGOs. It provided a definition of such NGOs as voluntary, independent, not-for-profit, and not self-serving. While these organizations are cherished and utilized by governments in many endeavours, they must remain independent of governments and are sometimes at odds with them. Their work received increasing recognition in CHOGM communiqués and in 1995, the Queen, in her speech at the heads of government banquet, praised the 'selfless' and 'unsung' work of the NGOs and suggested heads of government should support them by 'emulating their determination in pursuit of their objectives'. In Edinburgh, in 1997, she called them the 'soul and motor of the association'.[19]

The third level of NGOs are the sporting bodies, most notably the Commonwealth Games Federation, a body whose affiliates outnumber the Commonwealth members as remaining dependencies like the Cook Islands, St Helena and the Channel Islands are members. The Commonwealth Games emerged as the most popular and visible aspect of the Commonwealth, attracting over 2,000 competitors and 500 million television viewers.

The development of the Games mirrored the decolonization process. At the first British Empire Games in Hamilton, Canada, in 1930, competitors came from the British Isles and the Dominions, and only two Crown colonies, Bermuda and British Guiana. India did not send competitors until 1934, Nigeria and Malaya not until 1950. But by 1962, there were growing signs of African athletic prowess, which then flowered to produce fifty-two African medallists by 1974. Controversy over sporting contacts with South Africa by cricket and rugby football associations presented threats to the Games on various occasions. To this was added Britain's reluctance to apply sanctions against South Africa, which led to the disaster at Edinburgh in 1986 when more countries boycotted the Games than competed. Inequalities of development were evident in the distribution of sporting expertise and the fact that only one Games was held in a Third World Country – Jamaica in 1966.[20] Kuala Lumpur, however, was chosen as the venue for 1998.

Sporting inequalities led the Canadian Government to have the future of the Games placed on the agenda for the 1989 CHOGM in Kuala Lumpur. As a result, a Working Party on Co-operation Through Sport was created, chaired by a Canadian judge, Roy McMurtry. Over the next few years a series of eloquent reports from this group urged support for the Games and official financial backing to the Commonwealth Games Federation. Sport was seen as a popularizing and empowering instrument. 'Sport has an unparalleled ability to bring people together and ... to transcend cultural, linguistic and racial barriers.'[21] Sport is 'unparalleled in its ability to instil national unity and pride and build Commonwealth cohesion'. Passion for sport permeated societies from presidents and prime ministers to workers and school children. It served as 'the first point of information about the Commonwealth for young people'.[22]

An important part of this privatizing trend, therefore, was the fostering of a 'People's Commonwealth' made up of the non-governmental organizations through which hundreds of thousands of people participated in Commonwealth events. The styles 'Nonofficial Commonwealth' and 'NGO' have been deprecated as they define an important category of activity by what it is *not*. Some positive appellation has been sought, such as the American 'voluntary agencies', or Low's 'voluntary, professional and charitable organizations'.[23] Some comprehensive formulation encompassing voluntary, independent, professional, philanthropic and sporting organizations is required, but it is unlikely that the acronym VIPPSO will oust NGO. Whatever the appellation, their enduring significance was attested when the government of the People's Republic of China indicated that some of Hong Kong's NGO links might continue after the resumption of sovereignty in 1997, and the 1995 CHOGM announced that Nigeria's suspension did not apply to NGO links.

Fifty years after the end of the Raj, the Commonwealth, a key procedural instrument of British decolonization, had taken on a post-Britannic role which, perhaps, surprised the House of Commons inquiry by its utility and vitality, and 1997 was declared the 'Year of the Commonwealth' in Britain.

CONCLUSION

In the 1860s, when Britain was at its peak of wealth and power as the pioneer industrial nation, Charles Dilke toured the English-speaking world and in his book *Greater Britain* (brought out hastily in 1868) provided a powerful gloss on the mythology of Empire. In a section about 'dependencies', he said the tropical lands were 'a nursery of statesmen and warriors'[1] without which Britain would 'irresistibly fall into national sluggishness of thought'. India offered that 'vastness of dominion' which imparted 'width of thought and nobility of purpose'. Only forty years later, as rival powers already exceeded Britain in productive capacity and were competing in various parts of the world, Lord Curzon warned that when the Empire fell there would be poverty for many, 'narrow and selfish materialism' for others, and the country would be reduced to receiving flocks of tourists come to view castles, cathedrals and 'relics of a once mighty sovereignty' as they did at the ruins of Athens.[2] After another sixty years, Wilson's about-turn over East-of-Suez was, in Bernard Porter's words, 'momentous' as marking a watershed in Britain's long process of adjusting to the changing situation in the world.[3] In many respects, Dilke's and Curzon's prophecies had been fulfilled. But did the loss of Empire really bother the British?

We have seen how, in Whitehall, there had been agonizing over procedures, enunciation of 'never' categories, experiments with 'mezzanine' status, dismay that timetables were forever having to be scrapped, and disappointment that post-colonial democracy in many ex-colonies did not always approximate to the Westminster model. Yet, as Porter wrote, 'Decolonization went through on the nod.'[4] It was not a popular issue; it occasioned less regret than Britain's decline as a world power or its striking relative decline in economic performance compared with the new European partners such as Germany, France and Italy.

Returning to the questions posed in this book, summary answers must now be offered. In answering the question 'when?', we can see that the main landmarks came in the two decades between the Attlee decisions of 1947–8 and the Wilson decisions of 1967–8. At both these points,

Labour Governments were in power. But the chief watershed came in the aftermath of Suez, during the Macleod years, 1959–61 and, overall, Conservative Governments sent more dependencies to their independence than did Labour Governments. Winding up took another twenty years, but the withdrawal from East-of-Suez was the real end of Empire.

The answer to the 'why?' question has three parts, and my order of priority is, first, the impact of colonial nationalism, secondly, a structure of international relations which precluded old style colonialism and, thirdly, a realization in Britain that Empire was more a liability than an asset.

It has been admitted that the 'nationalist' forces sometimes proved to be flimsy constructions, but they played the key role in the timing of independence in particular cases. This stemmed from the long tradition of working with 'collaborators'. In the Dominions, power had long been handed over to elected local élites. In many Asian and African territories, Britain had ruled through various types of traditional élite. When local movements turned 'collaborators into critics'[5] the writing was on the wall. Although some parts of the Empire had been acquired by conquest and movements like 'Quit India', the Malayan communist insurrection and Mau Mau were restrained by force, terrorism in Palestine and Cyprus and warring factions in Aden became insurmountable problems. The British preferred a voluntary Empire to a repressive one. Thus, eventually, they always gave way to the nationalists.

The new structure of international relations emerged from the 1939–45 war. There were those who had predicted the effect of war. It was realized that Britain had only remained the major power between the wars by default and through the isolationism of the potential superpowers. Lord Vansittart said in 1940, 'it is better that the temple should perish and be remembered than be preserved and turned into a pig-sty'.[6] By 1945, Britain's reduction in wealth and strength compared to the USA and the USSR was all too evident. But the Empire had held and, for nearly a decade after the war, Britain remained ahead of the defeated axis powers and its own cross-Channel neighbours. By the mid-1950s, though, this position was blown. After Nasser's nationalization of the Suez Canal, Macmillan was remarkably uninhibited in private discussions with Americans. To Robert Murphy he said: 'If [we] had to go down now, the government and ... British people would rather do so on this issue than become perhaps another Netherlands.' And to President Eisenhower he even said, 'if the worst came to the worst they'd go down with bands playing, the guns firing, and the flags flying'. He felt Eisenhower did not understand, but Eisenhower was very clear about some things when he declared, thirty-five days later, 'I've just never seen Great Powers make such a complete mess and *botch* of things'.[7] It was Macmillan who, as chancellor of the exchequer, had to face the run on the pound and, as prime minister, would proclaim the 'Wind of Change' and, having missed the Treaty of Rome in 1957, would make belated supplication to the EEC in 1961.

By this time, the 'liability over asset' argument had come to the fore. Although Macmillan's profit and loss enquiry had been inconclusive in regard to particular dependencies, the superior economic growth of the European Six in the 1950s, as compared with the partly protected Commonwealth partners, indicated that Britain's trading needs were such that it could not stay aloof from Europe.

When we turn to the 'how?' question, decolonization has been seen as surprisingly peaceful. Britain was not ejected from its colonies by war, as Germany, Italy and Japan had been. The temporary losses in Southeast Asia were made good, even though prestige had been badly battered. The fall of the Empire was not accompanied by prolonged colonial wars and by domestic political and constitutional upheavals as in France in 1958 and Portugal in 1974.

The British Empire left an ambiguous legacy. On the one hand, there is the Commonwealth, which achieved a post-Britannic life of its own and enjoyed a considerable renaissance in the 1990s. On the other hand, there are some living cultural continuities. The English language became the fastest-growing language in the world – though not necessarily based on 'British-English'. There is also the popularity of the great team sports which were first codified in Victorian Britain and taught to the Empire and many other parts of the world – notably soccer, rugby and cricket. These are sports in which the British rarely compete as 'Britain' and, nowadays, do not often manage to win. This sporting world, with its passionate national rivalries, also reflects two of the more interesting aspects of the fall of the Empire.

First, as Linda Colley has suggested, imperial endeavours, especially warfare, made it easier for the English, Welsh, Scottish and Irish to do things in common. Empire was important in the making of 'Great Britain'. Now, if the component peoples of Britain are refocusing on their internal divisions, 'this conversely', she suggests, 'is part of the price they pay for peace and the end of world-power status'.[8] If Empire made Britain 'Great', will loss of Empire see it disintegrate? Or, more likely, will it contribute to a post-imperial Britain whose political structure is adjusted to reflect its tenacious traditional nationalities?

Secondly, a glance at sporting rivalries shows that some of the most accomplished sports performers are a reminder that the most visible legacies of Empire for the ordinary inhabitants of Britain are the Asian and Afro-Caribbean communities in their midst. A tradition of equal rights for British subjects, and full employment in the immediate post-war years, combined to encourage migration into the mother country in the last days of Empire. When, during the 'Wind of Change', Afro-Asian immigrants were found to be arriving at the rate of 100,000 a year and doubling every six months, there was a popular outcry for restrictions. To avoid charges of discrimination the first Commonwealth Immigration Act in 1962 was designed to apply to all Commonwealth migrants. But rigid controls were hard to enforce, the new Commonwealth communities were already well-established, and repatriation not an option. Thus the Empire's final bequest to post-imperial Britain was its modern multicultural society. With its lingering traditional nationalisms and efforts to Britannicize its newer ethnic communities, contemporary Britain faces, at home, some of the problems which its earlier rulers faced in attempting 'Dominion over palm and pine'.

NOTES AND REFERENCES

(Place of publication is London unless otherwise stated)

Abbreviations

BDEEP, A, 2, *Lab.*	R. Hyam (ed.), *British Documents on the End of Empire Project: The Labour Government . . . 1945–1951*, 4 vols. (HMSO, 1992)
BDEEP, A, 3, *Cons.*	D. Goldsworthy (ed.), *British Documents on the End of Empire Project: The Conservative Government . . . 1951–1957*, 3 vols. (HMSO, 1994)
BDEEP, B, 1, *Ghana*	R. Rathbone (ed.), *British Documents on the End of Empire Project: Ghana*, 2 vols. (HMSO, 1995)
BDEEP, B, 3, *Malaya*	A. J. Stockwell (ed.), *British Documents on the End of Empire Project: Malaya*, 3 vols. (HMSO, 1995)
BICAD	P. J. Cain and A. G. Hopkins, *British Imperialism: Crisis and Deconstruction 1914–1990* (Longman, 1993)
BIPAD	A. N. Porter and A. J. Stockwell (eds.), *British Imperial Policy and Decolonization 1938–1964*, 2 vols. (Macmillan, 1987)
BSFI	H. Tinker (ed.), *Constitutional Relations Between Britain and Burma. Burma: The Struggle for Independence 1944–1948*, 2 vols. (HMSO, 1983–4)
CAB	Cabinet papers, Public Record Office, London
CO	Colonial Office records, Public Record Office, London
Com.Sec.	The Commonwealth Secretariat
DAA	W. G. Morris-Jones and G. Fischer, *Decolonization and After: The British and French Experience* (Cass, 1980)
DAAI	P. Gifford and W. R. Louis, *Decolonization and African Independence: The Transfer of Power, 1960–1980* (New Haven: Yale University Press, 1988)
Darwin (1988)	J. Darwin, *Britain and Decolonisation: The Retreat from Empire in the Post-war World* (London: Macmillan, 1988)
Darwin (1991)	J. Darwin, *The End of the British Empire: The Historical Debate* (Oxford: Blackwell, 1991)
DO	Dominions Office and Commonwealth Relations Office records, Public Record Office, London

DRAF   J. Gallagher, *The Decline, Revival and Fall of the British Empire* ed.
                  by A. Seal (Cambridge University Press, 1982)
EOE   D. A. Low, *Eclipse of Empire* (Cambridge University Press, 1991)
Hancock   W. K. Hancock, *Survey of British Commonwealth Affairs*
(1937–42)   *1918–1936.* 2 vols. (Oxford University Press, 1937, 1942)
JCPS   *Journal of Commonwealth Political Studies* (Leicester University
                  Press)
JICH   *The Journal of Imperial and Commonwealth History* (Cass)
Louis (1977)   W. R. Louis, *Imperialism at Bay, 1941–1945: The United States
                  and the Decolonization of the British Empire* (Oxford: Clarendon
                  Press, 1977)
Louis (1984)   *The British Empire in the Middle East 1945–1951: Arab
                  Nationalism, the United States and Post-war Imperialism* (Oxford:
                  Clarendon Press, 1984)
Mansergh (1953)   N. Mansergh (ed.), *Documents and Speeches on British Common-
                  wealth Affairs, 1931–1952,* 2 vols. (Oxford University Press,
                  1953)
Mansergh (1958)   N. Mansergh, *Survey of British Commonwealth Affairs: Problems of
                  Wartime Co-operation and Post-war Change, 1939–1953* (Oxford
                  University Press, 1958)
Mansergh (1982)   N. Mansergh, *The Commonwealth Experience,* 2 vols.
                  (Macmillan, 1982)
Miller (1974)   J. D. B. Miller, *Survey of Commonwealth Affairs: Problems of
                  Expansion and Attrition 1953–1969* (Oxford University Press,
                  1974)
OUP   Oxford University Press
PMM   Commonwealth Prime Ministers' Meetings
PREM   Prime Ministers' papers, Public Record Office, London
Robinson (1972)   R. Robinson, 'Non-European foundations of European
                  imperialism: sketch for a theory of collaboration' in R. Owen
                  and B. Sutcliffe (eds.), *Studies in the Theory of Imperialism*
                  (Longman, 1972)
TOPA   P. Gifford and W. R. Louis, *The Transfer of Power in Africa:
                  Decolonization 1940–1960* (New Haven: Yale University Press,
                  1982)
TOPI   N. Mansergh *et al.* (eds.), *Constitutional Relations Between Britain
                  and India: The Transfer of Power, 1942–1947,* 12 vols. (HMSO,
                  1970–83)

Introduction: The Empire in 1946 and Decolonization

1. Order of march in WA II, 1: DA 327/18/2, New Zealand National
   Archives. See also *The Times,* 10 June 1946; *The Illustrated London News,* 15
   June 1946; *Picture Post,* 22 June 1946.

2. Louis (1984), p. 107.
3. M. J. Bonn, 'Imperialism' in *Encyclopedia of the Social Sciences* (New York: Macmillan, 1932), p. 612; *The Crumbling of Empire* (Allen & Unwin, 1938), pp. 101, 152, 235.
4. *The New Collins Concise Dictionary* (1982), p. 290.
5. *The Concise Oxford Dictionary* (8th ed., 1990), p. 301.
6. *The Oxford English Dictionary* (2nd ed., 1989), IV, p. 343.
7. J. D. Hargreaves, *Decolonization in Africa* (Longman, 1988), p. 2.
8. R. Robinson and J. Gallagher, 'The Partition of Africa' (1962) in *DRAF*, p. 72.
9. Introduction to *DAAI*, p. xxvi.
10. *JICH*, 1994, 22 (3): 462–511.
11. But see P. Lyon and J. Manor (eds.), *Transfer and Transformation: Political Institutions in the New Commonwealth* (Leicester University Press, 1983), p.1.
12. See BDEEP; *TOPI*; Darwin (1991); D. A. Low, 'Sequence and the Demission of Power', in *Lion Rampant* (Cass, 1973); minute by Poynton, 23 November 1959. CO 1036/331; Low, *EOE*; Louis, 'The Dissolution of the British Empire', in W. R. Louis and J. Brown (eds.), *The Oxford History of the British Empire*, IV (forthcoming); F. Ansprenger, *The Dissolution of the Colonial Empires* (Routledge, 1989); W. P. Kirkman, *Unscrambling an Empire . . . 1956–1966* (Chatto & Windus, 1966); Bonn, *The Crumbling of Empire*; C. Barnett, *The Collapse of British Power* (Eyre Methuen, 1972); C. E. Carrington, *The Liquidation of the British Empire* (Harrap, 1961); G. Balfour-Paul, *The End of Empire in the Middle East: Britain's Relinquishment of Power in her Last Three Arab Dependencies* (Cambridge University Press, 1991).
13. Gallagher, *DRAF*; see also C. Cross, *The Fall of the British Empire 1918–1968* (Paladin, 1970) and N. Tarling, *The Fall of Imperial Britain in South-East Asia* (Singapore: OUP, 1993).

PART I   When did the British Empire fall?

1. Darwin (1988), p. 334.
2. Louis, 'The Dissolution of the British Empire', in W. R. Louis and J. Brown (eds.), *The Oxford History of the British Empire*, IV (OUP, forthcoming), first paragraph.
3. Gallagher, *DRAF*, pp. 73, 153.
4. Austin, *TOPA*, pp. 225–47.

1   The Dominion Model

1. BDEEP, A, 2, *Lab.*, IV, p. 154. Psalm 72: 'dominion also from sea to sea and from the river unto the ends of the earth'. G. Martin, *Britain and the Origins of Canadian Confederation, 1837–67* (Macmillan, 1995), p. 282.

2. K. C. Wheare, *The Constitutional Structure of the Commonwealth* (Oxford: Clarendon Press, 1960), p. 8.

3. See J. M. Ward, *Colonial Self-Government: The British Experience 1759–1856* (Macmillan, 1976).

4. P. Burroughs, *The Canadian Crisis and British Colonial Policy, 1828–1841* (Arnold, 1922), p. 36.

5. C. Martin, *Empire & Commonwealth* (Oxford: Clarendon Press, 1929), p. 171.

6. C. P. Lucas (ed.),, *Lord Durham's Report in the Affairs of British North America* (Oxford: Clarendon Press, 1912), II, p. 278.

7. Grey to Harvey, 3 November 1846. W. P. M. Kennedy, *Statutes, Treaties and Documents of the Canadian Constitution 1713–1929* (OUP, 1930), p. 497.

8. S. R. Mehrotra, 'On the use of the term "Commonwealth"', *JCPS*, 1963 2 (1): 1–16.

9. Earl of Longford and J. P. O'Neill, *Eamon de Valera* (Hutchinson, 1970), pp. 130–73.

10. Text in J. Simmons (ed.), *From Empire to Commonwealth* (Odhams, 1949), p. 213.

11. Ibid., p. 225.

12. Note by Morris-Jones, 11 August 1947. *TOPI*, XII, pp. 664–6.

13. Mansergh (1958), p. 266.

2   The Attlee Government's Decisions of 1947–8

1. *TOPI*, I, pp. 4, 112.

2. For background see S. Wolpert, *A New History of India* (OUP, 1977); J. M. Brown, *Modern India* (OUP, 1985); C. H. Philips and M. D. Wainwright, *The Partition of India ...1935–47* (Allen & Unwin, 1970); J. Masselos, *Nationalism in the Indian Subcontinent* (Melbourne: Nelson, 1972); B. R. Tomlinson, *The Indian National Congress and the Raj, 1929–1942* (Macmillan, 1970); D. P. Singhal, *Pakistan* (Englewood Cliffs, NJ: Prentice-Hall, 1972).

3. *TOPI*, VII, pp. 334–5; see S. Ghosh, *Gandhi's Emissary* (Cresset Press, 1967).

4. *TOPI*, VII, pp. 416, 505.

5. Ibid., IX, pp. 427–30.

6. Ibid., p. 774.

7. Ibid., p. 957.

8. Ibid., X, p. 90.

9. Ibid., p. 191.

10. Ibid., p. 329.

11. Ibid., p. 699.

12. See below, pp. 107–9.

13. *BSFI*, II, p. 519.

14. Ibid., p. 573.

15. See below, pp. 111–12.

16. BDEEP, A, 2, *Lab*. I, p. 5.

17. Mansergh (1953), II, pp. 724, 751–2.
18. BDEEP, A, 2, *Lab.*, I, pp. 321–2.
19. See Stockwell, Introduction to BDEEP, B, 3, *Malaya*, I.
20. Ibid., II, p. 16.
21. Ibid., pp. 222–30.
22. See W. R. Louis and R. W. Stookey (eds.), *The End of the Palestine Mandate* (I. B. Tauris, 1980); Louis (1984), Chapter IV.
23. See R. Rathbone, Introduction to BDEEP, B, 1, *Ghana*, I.
24. A. H. M. Kirk-Greene, *The Principles of Native Administration in Nigeria* (OUP, 1965), pp. 193, 198, 200.
25. M. Perham, *Native Administration in Nigeria* (OUP, 1937), pp. 359–60.
26. R. Robinson, 'Andrew Cohen and the Transfer of Power in Tropical Africa, 1940–1951', *DAA*, p. 62; See also R. D. Pearce, *The Turning Point in Africa . . . 1938–48* (Cass, 1982), pp. 143–79.
27. BDEEP, A, 2, *Lab.*, I, p. 199.
28. Ibid., I, pp. 205–7.
29. R. Oliver, 'The Gamble for Africa', *Times Literary Supplement*, 9 April 1993, pp. 25–6.
30. Smaller Territories report, August 1951. DO 35/2218.

3   The Ambiguous Fifties

1. BDEEP, A, 3, *Cons.*, II, p. 2.
2. Ibid., I, p. 4.
3. Jeffries to Sedgwick, 31 March 1953. DO 35/5056.
4. Ibid., marginal note on Holmes to Sedgwick, 19 October 1953.
5. BDEEP, A, 3, *Cons.*, II, pp. 34, 42, 32.
6. *BIPAD*, II, p. 322.
7. BDEEP, B, 3, III, p. 226.
8. Ibid., III, p. 397.
9. Louis (1984), pp. 668–78.
10. W. S. Lucas, *Divided We Stand: Britain, the US and the Suez Crisis* (Hodder & Stoughton, 1991), p. 151.
11. Ibid., pp. 230–6.
12. M. Templeton, *Ties of Blood and Empire . . . 1947–57* (Auckland University Press, 1994), p. 102. See also J. Eayrs, *The Commonwealth and Suez* (OUP, 1964); W. R. Louis and R. Owen (eds.), *Suez 1956* (OUP, 1989) and W. J. Hudson, *Blind Loyalty: Australia and the Suez Crisis* (Melbourne University Press, 1989).

4   Macmillan and the 'Wind of Change', 1957–63

1. *BIPAD*, II, p. 451.
2. CP(O) (57)5, 30 May 1957. CAB 134/1551.

3. Ibid., CPC(57) 30(Revise), 6 September 1957.
4. Record of Final Session by Brook, 20 January 1958. PREM 11/2219.
5. CPC(59)2, 10 April 1959. CAB 134/1558.
6. Ibid., CPC(59) 1st mtg., 17 April 1959.
7. Cmnd. 814, p. 1.
8. *BIPAD*, II, pp. 525, 527, 528.
9. R. Shepherd, *Iain Macleod* (Hutchinson, 1994), p. 16.
10. See R. F. Holland, *European Decolonization 1918–1981* (Macmillan, 1985), pp. 153–90; R. F. Betts, *France and Decolonisation 1900–1960* (New York: St. Martin's Press, 1991), pp. 94–126.
11. CPC(61)1, 3 January 1961. CAB 134/1560.
12. For Mau Mau see B. Borman and J. Lonsdale, *Unhappy Valley* (Currey, 1992), Part V.
13. See J. Iliffe, *A Modern History of Tanganyika* (Cambridge University Press, 1979), chaps. 15, 16.
14. D. A. Low, *Political Parties in Uganda 1949–62* (Athlone Press, 1962); *Buganda in Modern History* (Weidenfeld and Nicolson, 1971); 'A Dislocated Polity: Uganda 1960–86' in *EOE*, pp. 312–25.
15. C. Palley, *The Constitutional History and Law of Southern Rhodesia 1888–1965* (Oxford: Clarendon Press, 1966), pp. 215–20.
16. See P. Short, *Banda* (Routledge & Kegan Paul, 1974); R. I. Rotberg, *The Rise of Nationalism in Central Africa* (Cambridge, Mass.: Harvard University Press, 1965).
17. Shepherd, *Macleod*, p. 221.
18. Note for the record by Bligh dated 20 July 1960 of meeting on 13 July. PREM 11/3649.
19. Report of Officials' Group, 23 July 1960. CAB 133/200.
20. Mills to Bligh, 11 December 1961. PREM 11/3654. On the significance of the Cyprus precedent see McIntyre, 'The Admission of Small States to the Commonwealth', *JICH*, 1996, 24(2): 244–77.
21. See D. Lowenthal (ed.), *The West Indies Federation* (New York: Columbia University Press, 1961); H. Springer, *Reflections on the Failure of the First West Indian Federation* (Cambridge, Mass.: Harvard University Press, 1962).
22. J. M. Gullick, *Malaysia* (Benn, 1969), pp. 163–78.
23. BDEEP, A,3, *Cons.*, I, pp. 228–31.
24. AT(NIG) 7, 31 December 1959. CAB 133/151; CPC(61)4, 27 February 1961. CAB 134/1560.

5   Wilson and the Withdrawal from East-of-Suez, 1966–76

1. *Labour Party: Report of 61st Annual Conference* (Transport House, 1962), p. 159.
2. B. Pimlott, *Harold Wilson* (HarperCollins, 1993), pp. 303–4.
3. G. Balfour-Paul, *The End of Empire in the Middle East* (Cambridge University Press, 1991), p. 84.

4. T. J. Spinner, *A Political and Social History of Guyana, 1945–1983* (Westview Press, 1984), pp. 67–128.
5. H. Wilson, *The Labour Government 1964–1970* (Weidenfeld and Nicolson, 1971), pp. 309–17, 575–7.
6. C. M. Turnbull, *A History of Singapore 1819–1975* (OUP, 1985), pp. 287–93.
7. See W. D. McIntyre, *Britain, New Zealand and the Security of South-East Asia in the 1970s* (Wellington: NZ Institute of International Affairs, 1969), pp. 7–18; P. Darby, *British Defence Policy East of Suez 1947–1968* (OUP, 1973), pp. 304–25.
8. Balfour-Paul, *End of Empire in the Middle East*, Chapter 3.
9. Ibid., Chapter 4.
10. See A. Smith, *Stitches in Time* (André Deutsch, 1981).
11. S. D. Wilson, 'Cook Islands Development 1946–65', in *New Zealand's Record in the Pacific Islands in the Twentieth Century*, ed. by A. Ross (Auckland: Longman Paul, 1969), pp. 84–114.
12. See B. Macdonald, *In Pursuit of the Sacred Trust* (Wellington, NZ Institute of International Affairs, 1988).

6 Closing the Files on the Pacific, Caribbean and Southern Africa

1. *The Commonwealth at the Summit* (Com.Sec., 1987), pp. 156–7.
2. Memo by Cohen, 2 March 1960; brief in Blair to Jerrom, 4 April 1960. CO 936/645.
3. Macmillan to SSCols, 16 June 1959. DO 35/8095.
4. Minute by Poynton, 23 November 1959. CO 1036/331.
5. J. V. Scott to R. C. Omerod, 12 October 1961. CO 1036/860.
6. Selkirk to Maudling, 30 November 1961 in PFP(62)3, 3 January 1962. CAB 134/2402.
7. Ibid., High Commissioner (Canberra) to CRO, 2 March 1962.
8. B. V. Lal, *Broken Waves* (Honolulu: University of Hawaii Press, 1992), pp. 186–217. See also Ahmed Ali, *Fiji: From Colony to Independence 1874–1970* (Suva: University of the South Pacific, 1977).
9. UK High Commission (Wellington), 30 March 1962 Extract in PFP(62)10, 6 April 1962. CAB 134/2402.
10. Ibid., Selkirk to Maudling, 30 November 1961.
11. Ibid., Selkirk to Maudling, 24 January 1962 in PFP(62)7, 12 February 1962.
12. B. Macdonald, 'Britain', in K. R. Howe *et al.* (eds.), *Tides of History* (Allen & Unwin, 1994), pp. 173–9.
13. I. C. Campbell, *Island Kingdom: Tonga Ancient & Modern* (Christchurch: Canterbury University Press, 1992), pp. 184–5, 193.
14. J. A. Bennett, *Wealth of the Solomons . . . 1800–1978* (Honolulu: University of Hawaii Press, 1987), pp. 311–43. See also H. Laracy (ed.), *Pacific Protest: The Maasina Rule Movement . . . 1944–52* (Suva: Institute of Pacific Studies, 1983).

15. B. Macdonald, *Cinderellas of the Empire* (Canberra: Australian National University Press, 1982), pp. 262–75.
16. H. Van Trease, *The Politics of Land in Vanuatu* (Suva: Institute of Pacific Studies, 1987), pp. 206–58.
17. *The Europa Year Book, 1987*, I, pp. 108–9; *What is CARICOM?* (Georgetown: Caribbean Community Secretariat, 1987).
18. See A.Verrier, *The Road to Zimbabwe 1890–1980* (Cape, 1986); J. Davidow, *A Peace in Southern Africa: The Lancaster House Conference on Rhodesia, 1979* (Westview Press, 1989); W. D. McIntyre, *The Significance of the Commonwealth, 1965–1990* (Macmillan, 1991), pp. 110–15.

PART II Why did the British Empire fall?

1. D. Austin, 'The British Point of No Return', *TOPA*, p. 225.
2. *DRAF*, p. 74.
3. R. Robinson, 'Andrew Cohen and the Transfer of Power in Tropical Africa', *DAA*, p. 56.
4. W. R. Louis and R. Robinson, 'The Imperialism of Decolonization', *JICH*, 1994 22(3): 462.
5. D. Birmingham, *The Decolonization of Africa* (UCL Press, 1995), p. 91.
6. *EOE*, p. xii.
7. Darwin (1988), p. 17.
8. Darwin (1991), pp. 5–7.

7 The Metropolitan Dimension

1. S. Howe, *Anticolonialism in British Politics . . . 1918–1964* (Oxford: Clarendon Press, 1993), p. 323.
2. D. Goldsworthy, *Colonial Issues in British Politics 1945–1961* (Oxford: Clarendon Press, 1971), pp. 375–6, 377–8, 385.
3. A. P. Thornton, 'Decolonization' in *For the File on Empire* (Macmillan, 1968), p. 356.
4. R. F. Holland, *European Decolonization 1918–1981* (Macmillan, 1985), p. 209.
5. Darwin (1991), p. 16.
6. Thornton, 'Decolonization', p. 349.
7. C. Barnett, *The Lost Victory* (Macmillan, 1995), pp. xii–xiii, 45.
8. W. D. Rubinstein, *Capitalism Culture and Decline in Britain 1750–1990* (Routledge, 1993), pp. 49, 52, 139.
9. P. Kennedy, *The Rise and Fall of the Great Powers* (Fontana, 1989), p. xxv.
10. Hancock (1937–42), II (1), p. 233.
11. A. Cairncross, *The British Economy since 1945* (Oxford: Blackwell, 1992), p. 45.

12. M. Ashton, 'Macmillan and the Middle East', in R. Aldous and S. Lee (eds.), *Harold Macmillan and Britain's World Role* (Macmillan, 1996), p. 37.
13. CPC(57) 30(Revise), 6 September 1957. CAB 134/1551.
14. D. Reynolds, *Britannia Overruled* (Longman, 1991), pp. 207–8.
15. Cairncross, *British Economy since 1945*, p. 84.
16. Louis (1984), p. 15.
17. P. Hennessy, *Never Again: Britain 1945–51* (Cape, 1992), p. 268.
18. Ibid., p. 221.
19. PMM (46) 1st mtg., 23 April 1946. CAB 133/86.
20. Darwin (1988), p. 334.
21. W. R. Louis and R. Robinson, 'The Imperialism of Decolonization', *JICH* 1994 22(3): 495.
22. N. Tarling, *The Fall of Imperial Britain in South-East Asia* (Singapore: OUP, 1993), pp. 2, 132.
23. *BICAD*, pp. 297–315. See also Reynolds, *Britannia Overruled*, pp. 2, 11–19; Rubinstein, *Capitalism, Culture, and Decline in Britain*, pp. 24–5, 31, 35.

8   The Global Dimension

1. Louis (1977), p. 129.
2. Ibid., p. 198.
3. Ibid., p. 200.
4. Ibid., p. 433.
5. Ibid., p. 458.
6. See below p. 118.
7. BDEEP, B, 2, *Ghana*, I, pp. 269–73; II, p. 392.
8. CC (53) 56th Concl. Minute 1, 8 October 1953. PREM 11/827; PMM (UK) (64)A.26. CAB 133/264.
9. C. M. Turnbull, *A History of Singapore 1819–1975* (OUP, 1985), pp. 277–8; B. W. and L. Y. Andaya, *A History of Malaysia* (Macmillan, 1982), pp. 270–5; V. Purcell, *Malaysia* (Thames & Hudson, 1965), pp. 185–202; J. M. Gullick, *Malaysia* (Benn, 1969), pp. 173–8.
10. Selkirk to Maudling, 30 November 1961. CAB 134/2402.
11. Ibid., UK High Commissioner, Wellington, 30 March 1962 in PFP(62)10, 6 April 1962.
12. See J. Davidow, *A Peace in Southern Africa: The Lancaster House Conference on Rhodesia, 1979* (Westview Press, 1989).
13. Minute for PM, 28 June 1950. PREM 11/2587.
14. W. R. Louis and R. Robinson, 'The Imperialism of Decolonization', *JICH*, 1994 22(3): 494.
15. *DRAF*, p. 90.
16. *EOE*, p. 7.

9 The Colonial Dimension

1. *BICAD*, p. 7.
2. R. Robinson, 'Andrew Cohen and the Transfer of Power in Tropical Africa, 1940–1951', in *DAA*, pp. 52, 59.
3. Ibid., p. 50; cf. 'Imperial Theory and the Question of Imperialism after Empire', JICH, 1984 12(2): 53.
4. *EOE*, pp. 262–3.
5. Preface to *DRAF*, p. x; 'Imperialism and Nationalism in India' in *Modern Asian Studies*, 1973 7(3): 345.
6. Ibid., pp. 324–5.
7. Ibid., p. 347.
8. *EOE*, pp. 297–311.
9. *DAA*, p. 11.
10. *TOPI*, IX, pp. 319, 358.
11. Ibid., X, p. 191.
12. *BSFI*, I, p. xv.
13. G. Balfour-Paul, *The End of Empire in the Middle East* (Cambridge University Press, 1991), pp. 76–95.

PART III   How did the British Empire fall?

1. *EOE*, p. 238.
2. Mansergh (1982), II, p. 240.
3. Darwin (1991), p. 2.
4. D. Reynolds, *Britannia Overruled* (Longman, 1991), p. 302.
5. Hancock (1937–42), I, p. 61.
6. N. Mansergh, *The Name and Nature of the British Commonwealth* (Cambridge University Press, 1955), p. 30.
7. Mansergh (1982), II, p. 240.
8. J. D. B. Miller, *The Commonwealth in the World* (Duckworth, 1965), p. 297; Miller (1974), p. 525.
9. D. Austin, 'The British Point of No Return' in *TOPA*, p. 247.
10. *BICAD*, p. 285.
11. *EOE*, pp. xiii, 332–3.

10   Transfers of Power

1. Menzies in conversations at Admiralty House, 24 June 1963. PREM 11/4096; Goldsworthy, *Colonial Issues*, p. 363.
2. *DRAF*, p. 65.

3. R. Robinson (1972), pp. 118, 138–9.
4. R. Robinson, 'Imperial Theory and the Question of Imperialism After Empire', *JICH* 1984 12(2): 47, 49.
5. W. R. Louis and R. Robinson, 'The Imperialism of Decolonization', *JICH*, 1994 22(3): 495.
6. Low, 'Sequence and the Demission of Power' in *Lion Rampant*, p. 170.
7. D. Austin, 'The British Point of No Return', *TOPA*, p. 235.
8. CR(48)5, 14 September 1948. CAB 134/118.
9. Attlee memo, 30 December 1948. BDEEP, A, 2, *Lab.*, IV, p. 178.
10. Brook to Syers, 19 July 1949; Syers to Brook, 3 August 1949. DO 35/2255.
11. Constitutional Development and Colonial Territories, 28 February 1951. DO 35/2217.
12. Minute by J. S. Bennett, 9 July 1954. CO 1032/50.
13. CM (44)5, 1 December 1955. BDEEP, A, 3, *Cons.*, II, p. 50; B, 2, *Ghana*, II, p. 214.
14. Footnote on Nomenclature, 8 July 1960, in Chadwick to Davies, 26 July 1960. DO 35/7877.
15. Brook for PM, 26 April 1960. PREM 11/3220.

11 Republics in the Commonwealth

1. See R. J. Moore, *Making the New Commonwealth* (Oxford: Clarendon Press, 1987).
2. *TOPI*, IX, pp. 31, 136, 304, 307.
3. Ibid., p. 917.
4. Ibid., XI, p. 124.
5. Ibid., X, pp. 609–10.
6. Governor-General of Malaya to Secretary of State for the Colonies (183) 27 June 1947 in CR(47)3, 15 September 1947. CAB 134/117.
7. BDEEP, A, 2, *Lab.*, IV, pp. 153–5.
8. CR(48), 2, 21 May 1948; CR(48), 2nd mtg., 31 May 1948. CAB 134/118.
9. Mansergh (1958), p. 283.
10. Record of meeting, 22 December 1948 with CR(49)1, 3 January 1949 CAB 134/119.
11. Ibid., memo of 31 December 1948.
12. Ibid., CR(49), 1st meeting, 7 January 1949.
13. Ibid., CR(49), 1st meeting, 11 January 1949; CR(49)2, 4 February 1949.
14. BDEEP, A, 2, *Lab.*, IV, pp. 187–92.
15. Noel Baker for PM, 20 April 1949. DO 121/23.
16. Gordon-Walker for PM, 6 April 1949. CAB 134/119.
17. Ibid., CR(49)15, 9 April 1940; CR(49) 7th meeting, 8 April 1949.
18. Mansergh (1958), p. 286.

19. PMM (49) 1st meeting, 22 April 1949. CAB 133/89.
20. PMM (UK) (49)1, 25 April 1949. CAB 133/91 on meeting of 22 April.
21. Communiqué, 26 April 1949, in *The Commonwealth at the Summit* (Com.Sec., 1987), p. 29.
22. PMM (49) 6th meeting, 27 April 1949. CAB 133/89.

12   The Commonwealth: Disillusionment, Detachment and Rediscovery

1. BDEEP, A, 3, *Cons.*, II, pp. 5–6.
2. Minute by Chadwick, 9 January 1957. DO 35/5011.
3. Macmillan to Menzies (Secret & Confid.), 8 February 1962. PREM 11/3649.
4. Ibid., Brook for PM, 6 February 1962.
5. A. Smith, *Stitches in Time* (André Deutsch, 1981), pp. 4–6; W. D. McIntyre, *The Significance of the Commonwealth* (Macmillan, 1991), pp. 47–51.
6. Auckland Communiqué, 1995, in *The Commonwealth Yearbook, 1996,* pp. 41–53.
7. McIntyre, *Significance of the Commonwealth*, p. 56.
8. Ibid., p. 62; S. Ramphal, *One World to Share* (London: Hutchinson Benham, 1979), p. 224.
9. House of Commons, Foreign Affairs Committee, Examination of Witnesses on FCO Memo, 7 June 1995, p. 15.
10. Communiqué, 26 April 1949, *The Commonwealth at the Summit* (Com.Sec., 1987), pp. 156–7.
11. *Seventh Report of Secretary-General* (Com.Sec., 1979), p. 6.
12. *Commonwealth Yearbook, 1996,* pp. 103–9.
13. *Towards a Commonwealth of Learning* (Com.Sec., 1987), p. 50.
14. *The Commonwealth Foundation: A Special Report 1966–1993* (Marlborough House, 1993), pp. 4–10.
15. W. D. McIntyre, 'End of an era for the Commonwealth: thoughts on the Hibiscus Summit', *NZ International Review*, 1990 15(1): 6.
16. House of Commons, Session, 1995–96, Foreign Affairs Committee: *The Future Role of the Commonwealth* (HMSO, 1996), p. 1xix.
17. Harare Declaration, 1991, para.9. *Commonwealth Yearbook, 1996*, p. 105.
18. See McIntyre, *Significance*, Chapter 11.
19. Press releases of texts, 10 November 1995, 24 October 1997.
20. McIntyre, *Significance*, Chapter 13; C. Dheensaw, *The Commonwealth Games . . . 1930–1990* (Victoria, BC: Orca, 1994).
21. *Working Party on Strengthening Commonwealth Sport, Final Report* (Com.Sec., 1991), p. 10.
22. *CHOGM Committee on Co-operation Through Sport, 1993 Report* (Com.Sec., 1993), pp. xvii, 24.
23. *EOE*, p. 336.

Conclusion

1. C. W. Dilke, *Greater Britain* (Macmillan, 1868), II, pp. 394–5, 407.
2. B. Porter, *Britannia's Burden . . . 1851–1990* (Arnold, 1994), p. 124.
3. Ibid., p. 323.
4. Ibid., p. 301.
5. A. Seal, *The Emergence of Indian Nationalism* (Cambridge University Press, 1968), p. 23.
6. Porter, *Britannia's Burden*, p. 231.
7. W. S. Lucas, *Divided We Stand: Britain, the US and the Suez Crisis* (Hodder & Stoughton, 1991), pp. 150, 211, 270.
8. L. Colley, *Britons . . . , 1707–1837* (Pimlico, 1992), p. 164.

INDEX

partition
   India, 26–7
   Ireland, 17, 19
   Palestine, 32
Patel, Vallabhbhai, 25
Pearce, Lord, 75
Penang, 30
People's Commonwealth, 128
People's Republic of South Yemen, 64
Perham, Margery, 34
Persian Gulf, *see* Arabian/Persian Gulf
Philippines, 93
Pitcairn, 6
Port Said, 5, 43
Porter, Bernard, 129
Portuguese Empire, 75–6, 92, 93, 99, 105
Powell, Enoch, 120
Prime Ministers' Meetings,
   Commonwealth
   (1946), 87, 91
   (1948), 107, 113
   (1961), 120
   (1964), 91, 120–1
   see also Heads of Government
      Meetings
Prince Edward Island, 16
Princely States, Indian, 1, 2, 21, 23, 33
profit and loss analysis, Macmillan's, 45, 93
Protected States
   Arabian/Persian Gulf States, 5, 64–5
   Brunei, 3, 55, 63
   Malay States, 3, 30, 33
   Tonga, 6, 37, 68, 71
   Zanzibar, 5, 56
   see also Princely States, Indian

Qatar, *x*, 5, 64–5
Queen Victoria, 16, 21
Queen Elizabeth II, 127
   see also Head of the Commonwealth
Quit India movement, 24, 130

Rabi Island, 72

Ramphal, Sonny, 122, 124–5
Rance, Governor, 28, 98, 111
Red Sea, 5
regional organizations, 123
representative government, 14–15
responsible government
   Burma, 27
   Ceylon, 29
   evolution of, 13–14, 106
   incremental route to, 35, 59, 106
Reynolds, David, 101
Robinson, Kenneth, 35
Robinson, Ronald, 7, 8, 35, 79, 87, 94, 95, 96, 103–4
Roosevelt, President, 24, 90
Ross Dependency, 6
Round Table Conference, Indian, 22–3, 105
Royal Title, 27, 118
Rubinstein, W. D., 82

Sabah, *ix*
   see also British North Borneo
St Helena, 1, 4
St Kitts and Nevis, *x*, 4, 66, 73
St Lucia, *x*, 4, 66, 73
St Vincent and the Grenadines, *x*, 4, 66, 73
Sarawak, *ix*, 1, 3, 54
Sargent, Sir Orme, 110
Seal, Anil, 96
Second World War, *xi*, 1–2, 5, 6, 20, 130
Secretary-General, Commonwealth
   Arnold Smith, 65, 74, 122, 124
   Sonny Ramphal, 122–3
   Emeka Anyaoku, 124
Selkirk, Lord, 70–1
Senanayake, Don Stephen, 3, 29
Senghor, Leopold, 7
Seychelles, *x*, 1, 5, 63–4
Shanghai, 3
Sharpeville, 60
Shawcross, Sir Hartley, 26
Sierra Leone, *ix*, 4